Spanish Made Easy

Authors Reyes Ávila, Charlotte Tomson
Consultant José Manuel Verdú

DK

DK London
Editor Elizabeth Blakemore
Senior Editor Cécile Landau
Managing Editor Christine Stroyan
Managing Art Editor Anna Hall
Spanish Consultant José Manuel Verdú
Senior Production Editor Andy Hilliard
Senior Production Controller Jude Crozier
Jacket Design Development Manager Sophia MTT
Publisher Andrew Macintyre
Associate Publishing Director Liz Wheeler
Art Director Karen Self
Publishing Director Jonathan Metcalf

DK Delhi
Senior Editor Rupa Rao
Editor Rohini Deb
Art Editor Rashika Kachroo
Managing Editors Soma B. Chowdhury, Kingshuk Ghoshal
Managing Art Editor Govind Mittal
DTP Designers Anita Yadav, Rakesh Kumar, Harish Aggarwal
Senior Jacket Designer Suhita Dharamjit
Jackets Editorial Coordinator Priyanka Sharma

This edition published in 2020
First published in Great Britain in 2014 by
Dorling Kindersley Limited
DK, One Embassy Gardens,
8 Viaduct Gardens, London, SW11 7BW

10 9 8 7 6 5 4 3 2 1
015–196496–May/2020

A CIP catalogue record for this book is available from the British Library.
ISBN 978-1-4093-4938-9

Printed and bound in Great Britain by Bell and Bain Ltd, Glasgow

For the curious

www.dk.com

Contents

This chart lists all the topics in the book. Once you have completed each page, colour in a star in the correct box below.

¡Hola! ¿Cómo te llamas?

Say the following Spanish phrases out loud.

¡Hola!	¿Cómo te llamas?	Me llamo...
Hello!	What's your name?	I'm/My name is...

Look at the pictures below. Then read out the pairs of greetings in the box on the left. Write the correct pair for each picture in the speech bubbles.

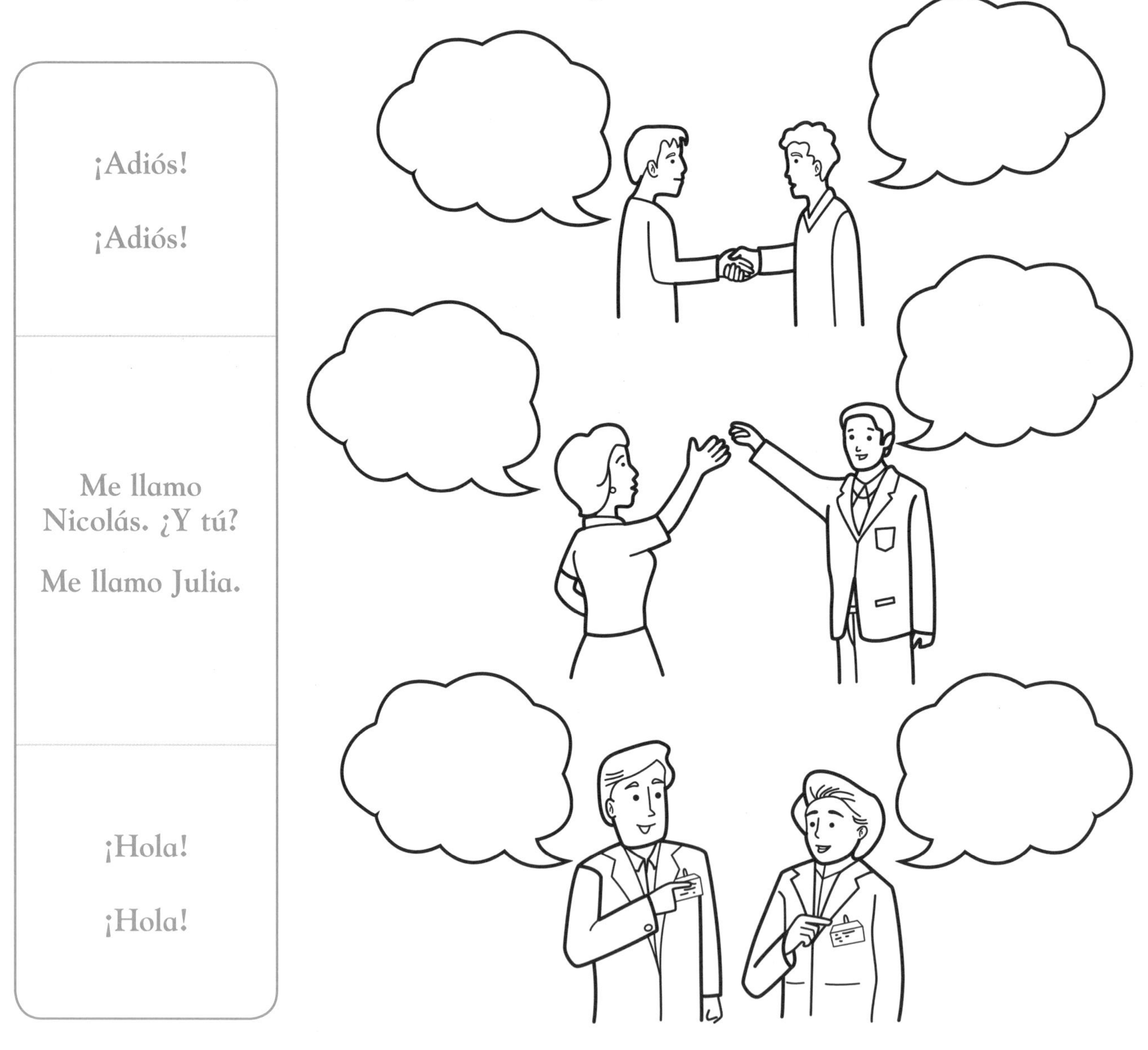

Here are two different ways of asking what someone's name is, but the vowels are missing. Can you supply them?

¿C.... m.... t.... ll.... m.... s?

¿C........ l .... s t.... n.... mbr.... ?

Señor Buho says, "Remember that in Spanish we write a question mark at the beginning as well as at the end of the sentence."

Look at these Spanish expressions.

¿Qué tal?	**Bien.**	**Muy bien, gracias.**	**No muy bien.**
How are you?	Fine.	Very well, thanks.	Not too well.

Now draw three faces in the box below: one happy and smiling, another looking sad and a third face that simply looks content and relaxed.
Choose an expression from above to match each of the faces you have drawn.

¿Y tú? ¿Qué tal?

....

Señor Buho says, "In Spanish, we also have a slightly more formal way of saying *How are you?* **We say,** *¿Cómo estás?*"

Los números 1–20

Point to each balloon and read the number on it out loud.

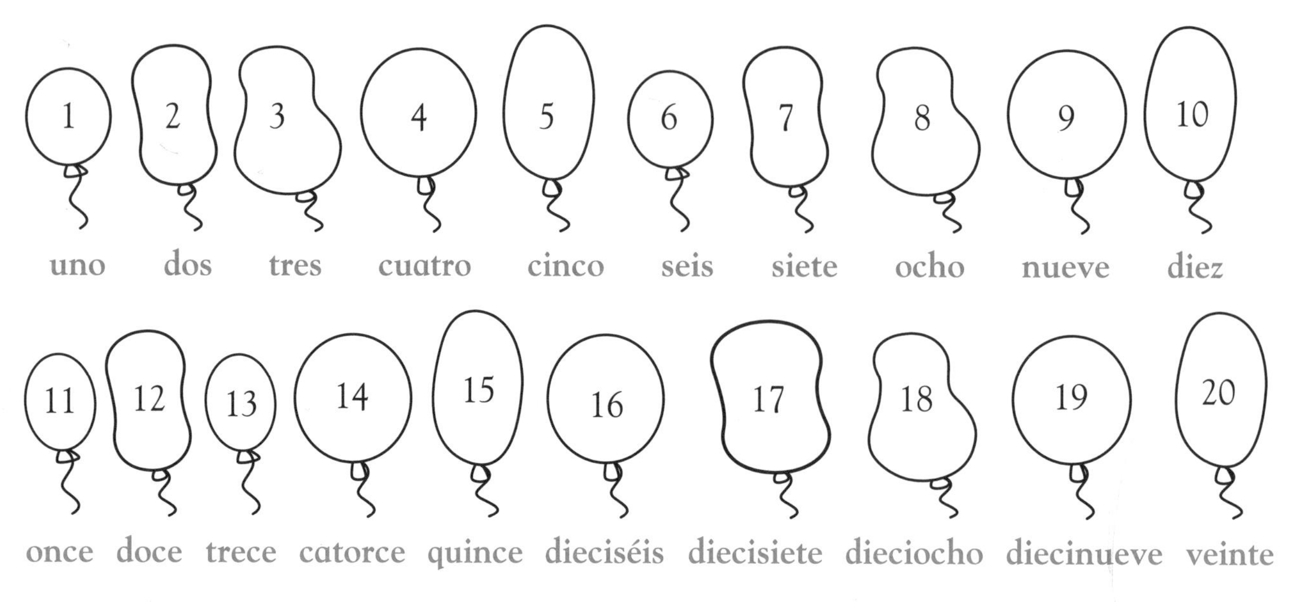

In the pictures below, numbers are shown in everyday situations.
Write the Spanish word for each number shown below the pictures.

Señor Buho says, "Keep revisiting numbers. Go for a number walk. Every time you spot a number, say it in Spanish."

¿Cuántos años tienes?

Read these useful Spanish sentences. Practise using them with family and friends, changing the number to match individual ages.

¿Cúantos años tienes?
How old are you?

Tengo diez años.
I am ten.

Tengo cinco años.
I am five.

Tengo dieciséis años.
I am sixteen.

Look at these pictures of people celebrating their birthdays.
Fill in the gaps in the speech bubbles.

The words in the sentences below have been mixed up. Rewrite the sentences with the words in the correct order.

1. seis años. Tengo ....

2. años. Tengo doce ....

3. Tengo años. catorce ....

4. diecinueve Tengo años. ....

Señor Buho says, "Remember to draw a little line over the 'n' in *años*. This letter is called an eñe."

En mi estuche

Look at these pictures and read out the labels. Say what you have in your pencil case.

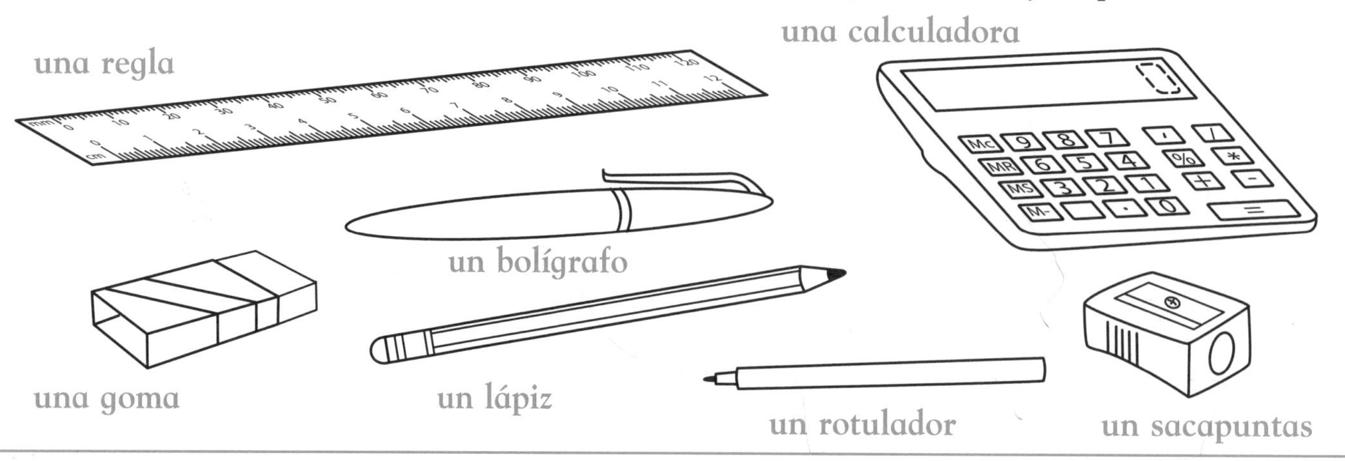

These children are describing the contents of their pencil cases.
Read each description and match it to the correct group of objects shown below.

In Spanish, all nouns (things or people) are either masculine or feminine. The Spanish word for *a* is either *un* or *una*, depending on whether the noun following it is masculine or feminine.

Put the words below in the correct place on the chart.

un bolígrafo, una goma,
una regla, un lápiz,
un rotulador, una calculadora

Masculine	Feminine
un boigrafo	una goma
un lápiz	una regular
un rotulador	una calculadora

Los adjetivos ★

Adjectives are used to describe people or things. Here are some useful Spanish adjectives you may use to describe yourself or your friends.

simpático/simpática

pequeño/pequeña

glotón/glotona

hablador/habladora

perezoso/perezosa

deportista

Answer the following question. Use any adjectives you know, including those given above, in your reply.

¿Cómo eres? Soy ....

What are you like? I am ....

Remember that adjectives in Spanish 'agree' with the object or person they are describing. Fill in the missing words on the chart below.

English	Masculine Adjective	Feminine Adjective
....	deportista	....
....	....	perezosa
talkative	....	....
small	....	....
....	....	glotona
nice	....	....

Los meses del año

Read out the list of months in the box on the right. Then look at the pictures below. Circle the month that best matches each picture.

Read these sentences.

Mi cumpleaños es el 4 de julio.
My birthday is on the 4th of July.

El cumpleaños de Sofía es el 8 de febrero.
Sofía's birthday is on the 8th of February.

Now look at the notes from a Birthday Book on the left.
Use the information given to complete these sentences.

BIRTHDAYS

Julie 18th March	*David 17th August*
Thomas 4th June	*Sam 10th May*

El cumpleaños de Julie es ....

El cumpleaños de Thomas es ....

El cumpleaños de David es ....

El cumpleaños de Sam es ....

¿Y tú? ¿Cuándo es tu cumpleaños?
And you? When is your birthday?

....

Señor Buho says, "In Spanish, months begin with a small letter, for example, *abril*. English uses a capital letter, for example, *April*."

Read out the times shown on the clock faces below.

Son las siete.	**Son las siete y cuarto.**	**Son las once y media.**	**Son las nueve menos cuarto.**

Read each sentence. Then circle the clock face above it showing that time.

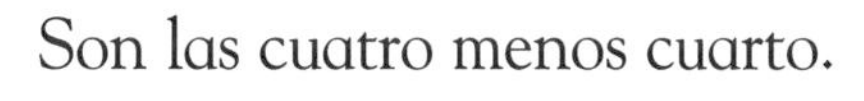

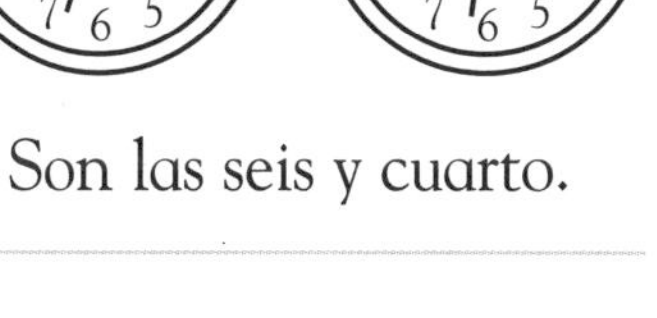

Son las dos y media. Son las cuatro menos cuarto. Son las seis y cuarto.

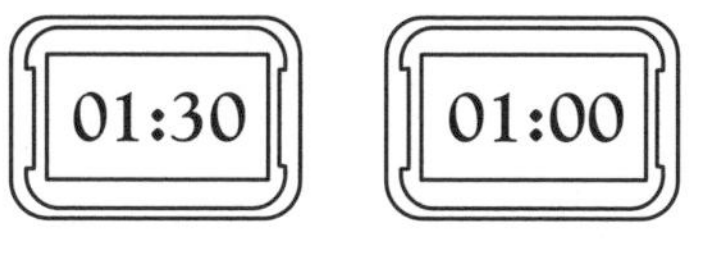

Son las dos. Son las nueve menos cuarto. Es la una y media.

Look at the phrases and pictures below.

a mediodía	**a las once**	**a las cinco y cuarto**	**a medianoche**
at midday	at eleven o'clock	at quarter past five	at midnight

Me despierto. **Me lavo.** **Desayuno.** **Me lavo los dientes.**

Read the sentences below, describing regular morning activities. The times given are unusual. Rewrite each sentence, using times that match your morning routine.

Me despierto a las once. ....

Me lavo a las once y media. ....

Desayuno a mediodía. ....

Me lavo los dientes a las cinco y cuarto. ....

Los colores

Here is a list of colours.

blanco	white	**amarillo**	yellow	**marrón**	brown
negro	black	**verde**	green	**gris**	grey
azul	blue	**rosa**	pink	**naranja**	orange
rojo	red	**morado**	purple		

Read the names of the colours out loud, then select from them to complete the sentences below.

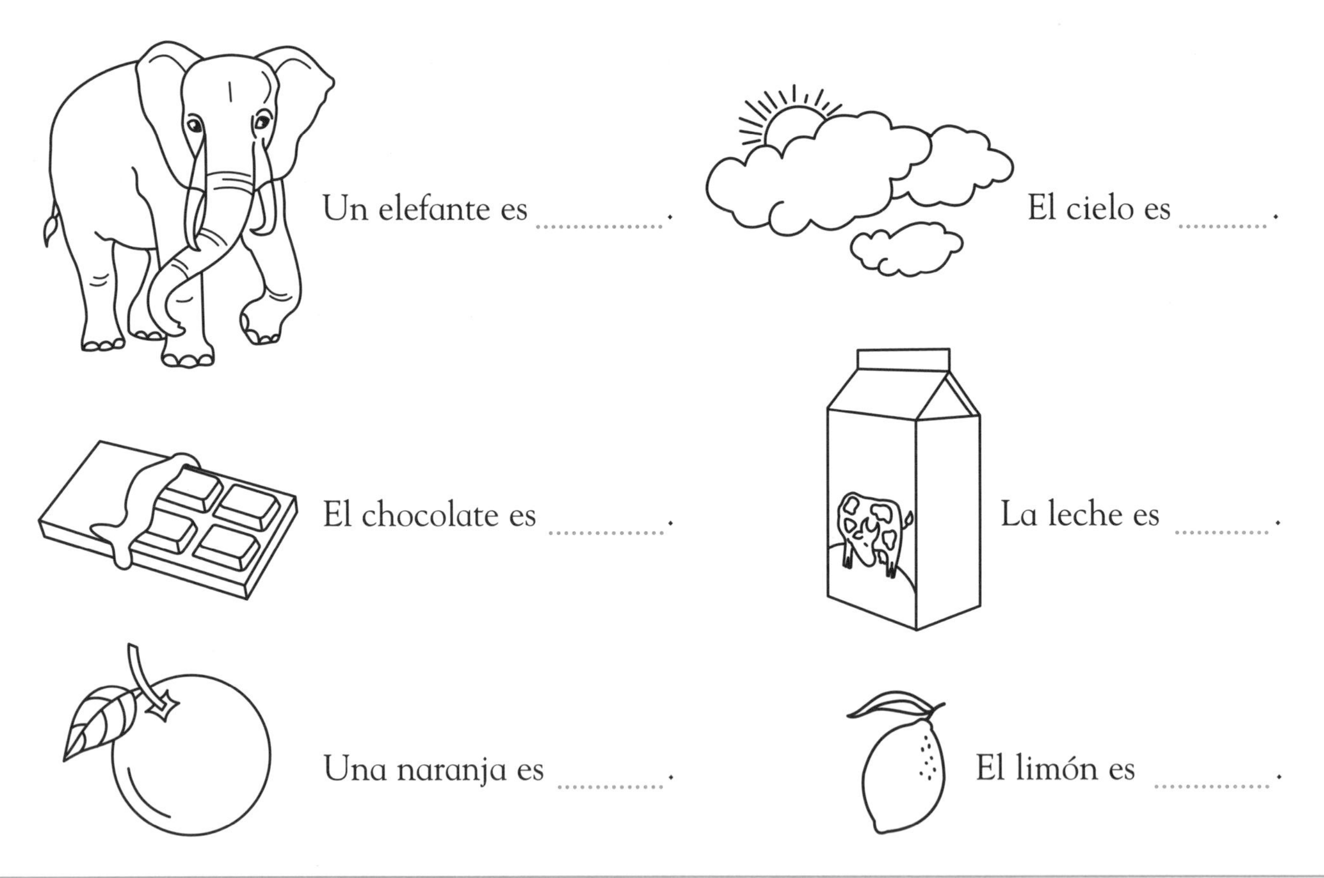

Un elefante es ....

El cielo es ....

El chocolate es ....

La leche es ....

Una naranja es ....

El limón es ....

Answer the following question.

¿Cuál es tu color favorito? Mi color favorito es ....

What is your favourite colour? My favourite colour is ....

Señor Buho says, "Compare new Spanish words with English words. Sometimes there are similarities that can help you remember them."

In Spanish, colours go after the noun they describe. They must also be written in either their masculine or feminine form, depending on whether the noun is masculine or feminine.

un lápiz negro	**una goma negra**
a black pencil	a black rubber

Fill in the gaps to reveal the objects and their colours.
You can look at pages 8 and 12 for any words you need.

1. A blue pen = u... bol.......afo a.......
2. A blue ruler = un... r.......a l
3. A black sharpener = un sa.........nt...... ne.......
4. A black rubber = una ......m... n.......a

Draw lines linking the masculine and feminine forms of each colour listed.

Masculine	Feminine
marrón	azul
azul	amarilla
verde	marrón
rojo	rosa
blanco	roja
amarillo	morada
rosa	verde
morado	negra
gris	blanca
negro	naranja
naranja	gris

Which colours stay the same? ....

Which colours change 'o' to 'a' to change from the masculine to feminine form? ....

El cuerpo

Read the following words out loud. As you say each word, touch that part of your body.

el brazo (plural: **los brazos**)	arm	**el pie** (plural: **los pies**)	foot	**la cabeza**	head
la pierna (plural: **las piernas**)	leg	**la oreja** (plural: **las orejas**)	ear	**la boca**	mouth
la rodilla (plural: **las rodillas**)	knee	**la mano** (plural: **las manos**)	hand	**la barriga**	tummy
el ojo (plural: **los ojos**)	eye	**el hombro** (plural: **los hombros**)	shoulder	**la nariz**	nose

Use the words above to label the figure shown below.

Add 's' or 'es' to an adjective, such as a colour, if you are using it to describe more than one thing.

Tiene los ojos azules.
He has blue eyes.

Tiene las piernas largas.
He has long legs.

Read these sentences describing a monster. Circle the correct adjective to use in each case.

La cabeza es amarillo / amarilla.

Tiene los ojos azules / azul.

La boca es negro / negra.

Tiene cuatro brazos azules / azul.

La barriga es roja / rojo.

Tiene las piernas verdes / verde.

Tiene las orejas pequeño / pequeñas.

Now draw and colour the monster described.

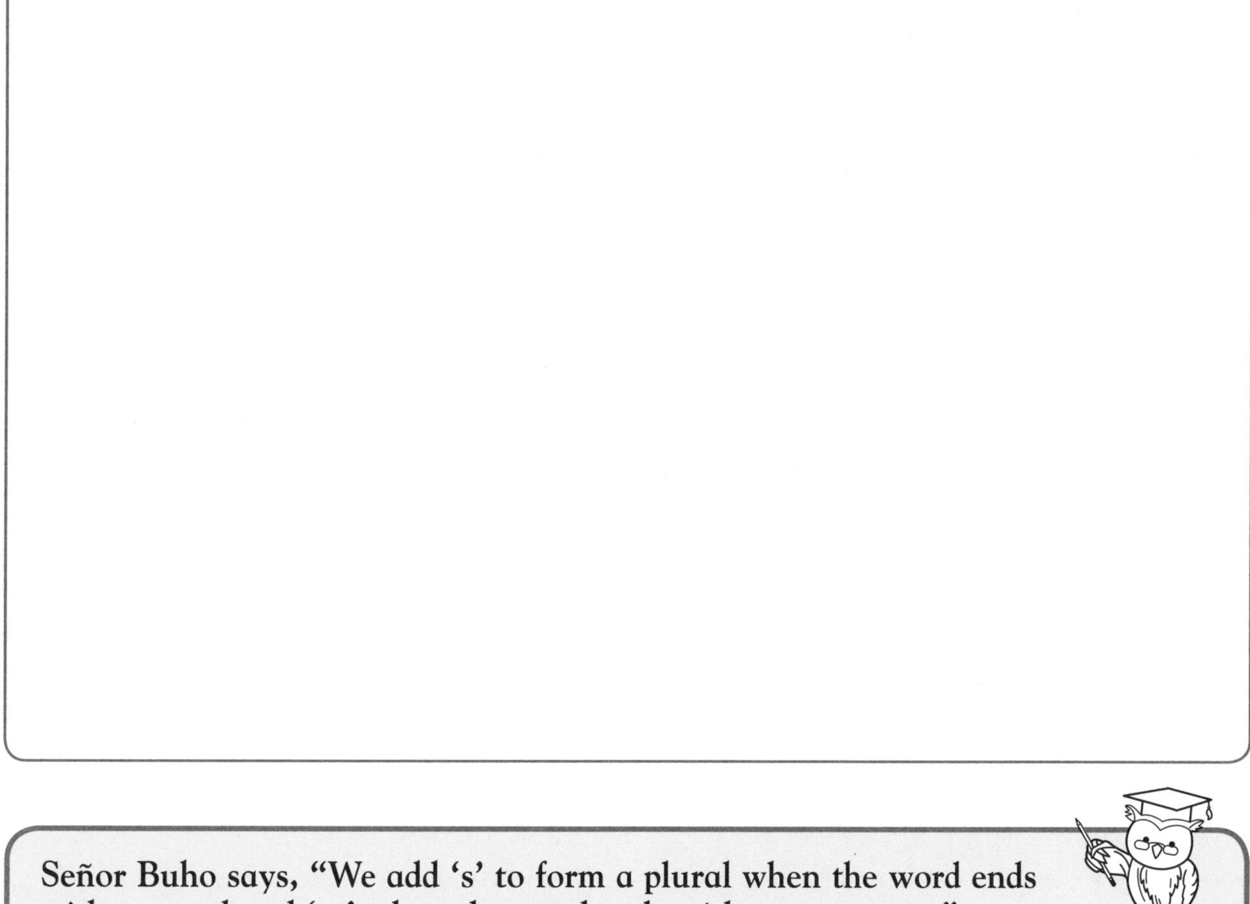

Señor Buho says, "We add 's' to form a plural when the word ends with a vowel and 'es' when the word ends with a consonant."

Los retratos

Read out the following Spanish sentences and phrases.

Tiene los ojos marrones. He has/She has brown eyes.	**los ojos verdes** green eyes	**los ojos azules** blue eyes
Tiene el pelo rubio. He has/She has blonde hair.	**el pelo negro** black hair	**Tiene barba.** He has a beard.
Lleva gafas. He/She wears glasses.	**el pelo corto** short hair	**el pelo largo** long hair

Now imagine you are the manager of a new pop band, *Los Tres Amigos*. Look at the picture below. Then use the words in the box under the picture to fill in the gaps in the description of your band members.

barba   largo   corto   y   gafas

pelo   Ella   tiene   ojos

Cristina tiene los ojos azules y el pelo .... y rubio. Pedro tiene los .... marrones y el .... corto y negro. Tiene .... Silvia .... los ojos verdes .... el pelo marrón y .... lleva ....

Read the following words and phrases.

mi padre my father	**mi madre** my mother	**Se llama...** He/She is called...	**Se llaman...** They are called...
un hermano a brother	**una hermana** a sister	**No tengo hermanos.** I don't have any sisters or brothers.	
Soy... I am...	**Es...** He is...	**Es...** She is...	

Read this extract from a letter to a penpal. Then decide if the statements on the chart are true (*verdadero*) or false (*falso*). Tick (✓) the right column. Look up any words you do not know in a dictionary or on the Internet.

En mi familia hay cinco personas. Mi padre se llama Pedro. Es alto y divertido. Mi madre, Susana, es baja y habladora. Tengo dos hermanas que se llaman Sofía y Julia. Sofía tiene cinco años y es tímida. Julia tiene nueve años. Julia tiene el pelo rubio y largo. ¡Es muy perezosa! Para terminar, me llamo David. Tengo siete años. Tengo los ojos verdes y llevo gafas. Mi cumpleaños es el once de julio. Soy deportista y un poco glotón. ¿Y tú? ¿Tienes hermanos?

	Verdadero	Falso
1. There are 4 people in the family.		
2. The father is called Pedro.		
3. The mother is talkative.		
4. David has a sister and a brother.		
5. Sofía is 9 years old.		
6. Julia has long blonde hair.		
7. Julia is shy.		
8. David is a bit greedy.		
9. David has blue eyes and wears glasses.		
10. David's birthday is on 11 July.		

Señor Buho says, "There are two different ways of saying *my*. Use *mi* in front of a singular noun and *mis* in front of a plural noun."

¿Tienes un animal?

Look at the pictures of the different animals below. Read out the Spanish word for each animal as you look at its picture.

un perro

un gato

un caballo

un ratón

un pájaro

un conejo

Translate the English clues and complete the crossword puzzle.

Across

1. bird ....
2. horse ....
3. mouse ....

Down

1. rabbit ....
2. cat ....
3. dog ....

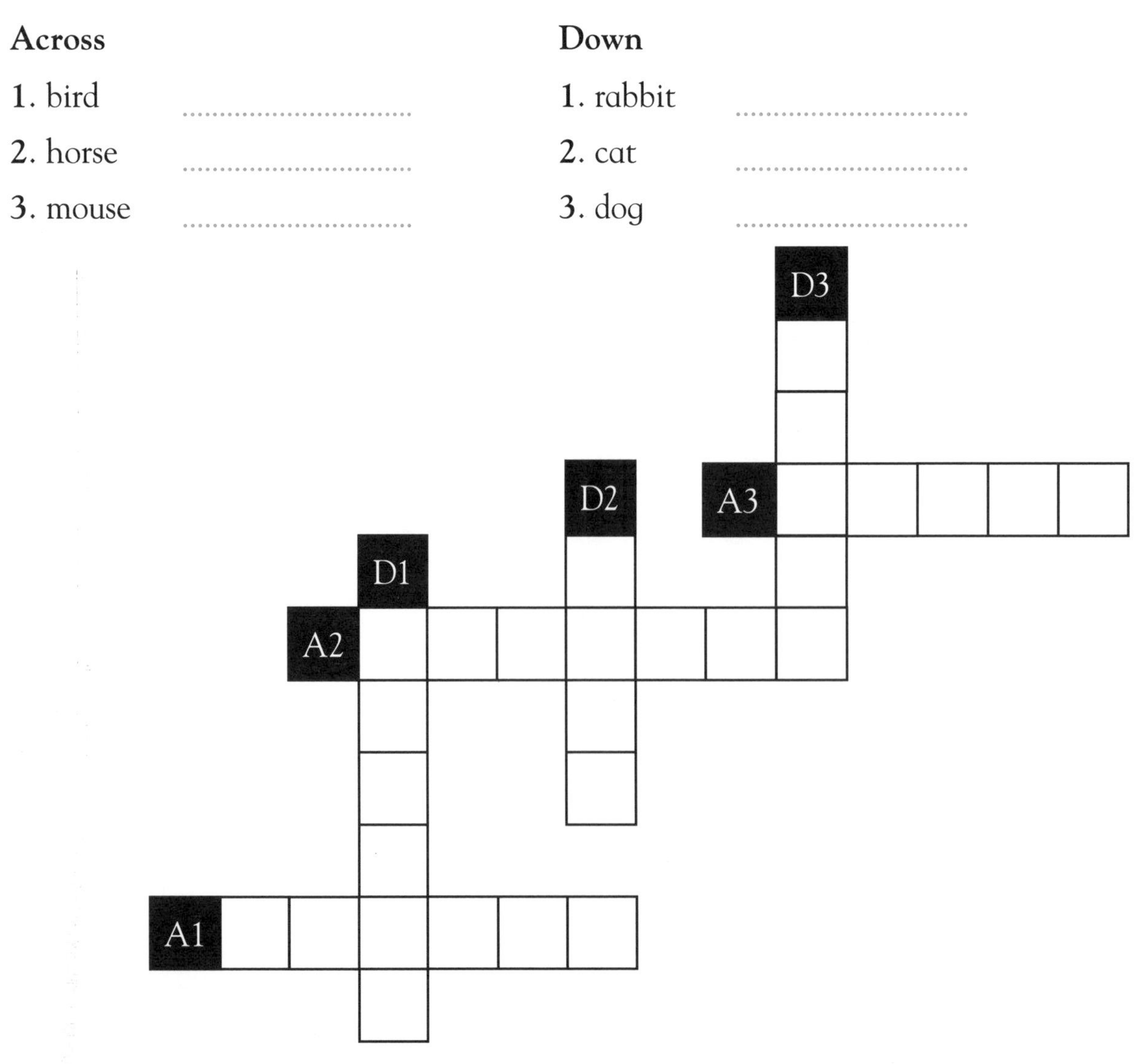

Most Spanish plurals are formed by adding an 's' when the word ends with a vowel and 'es' when the word ends with a consonant.

Look at the Spanish words illustrated below. Fill in the plural of each.

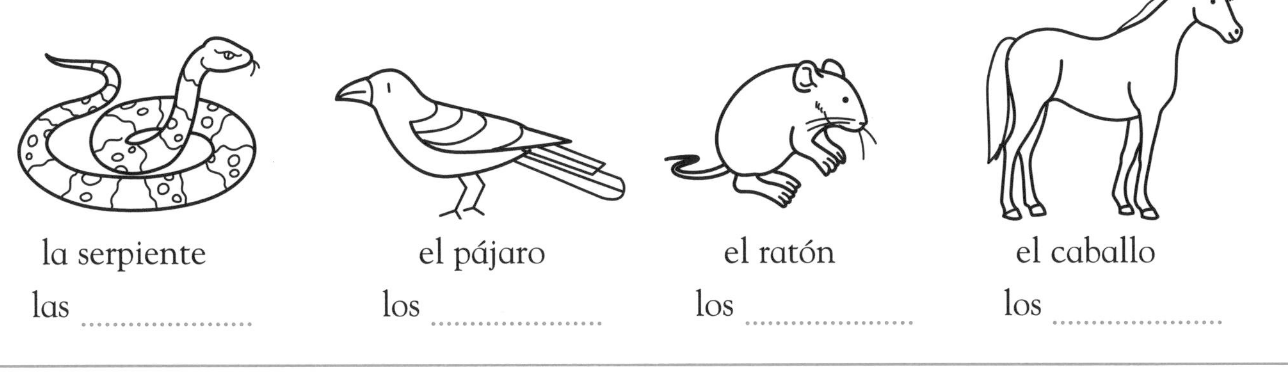

la serpiente — las ....

el pájaro — los ....

el ratón — los ....

el caballo — los ....

Look at this key.

Me gusta/gustan
I like

Me gusta/gustan mucho
I really like

Me encanta/encantan
I love

No me gusta/gustan
I don't like

Now use the key and the drawings below to build sentences.
The first one has been done for you.

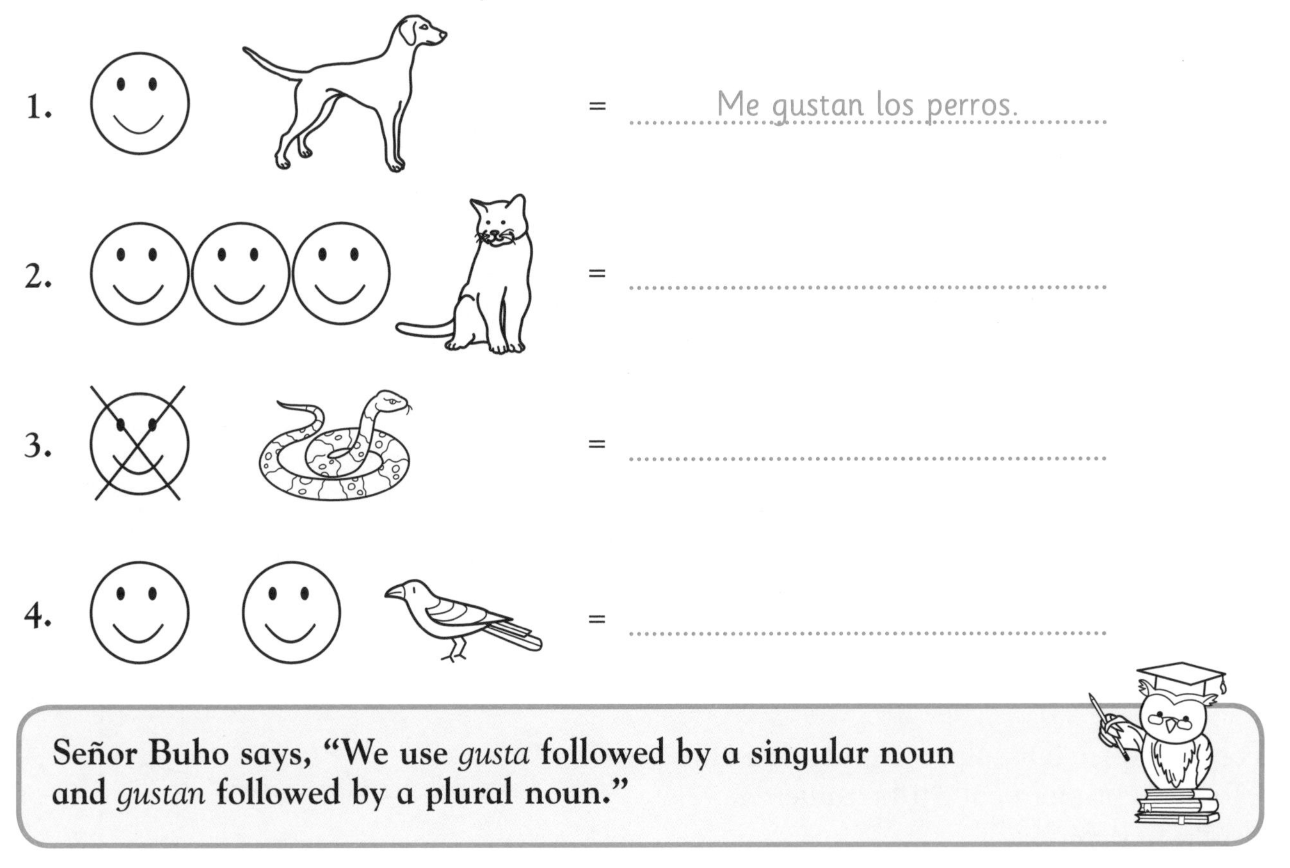

1. = Me gustan los perros.
2. = ...
3. = ...
4. = ...

Señor Buho says, "We use *gusta* followed by a singular noun and *gustan* followed by a plural noun."

¿Dónde está?

Look at the picture. The pets in this house are on the loose! Use the labels and position words in the box on the right to fill in the gaps in the description of the scene.

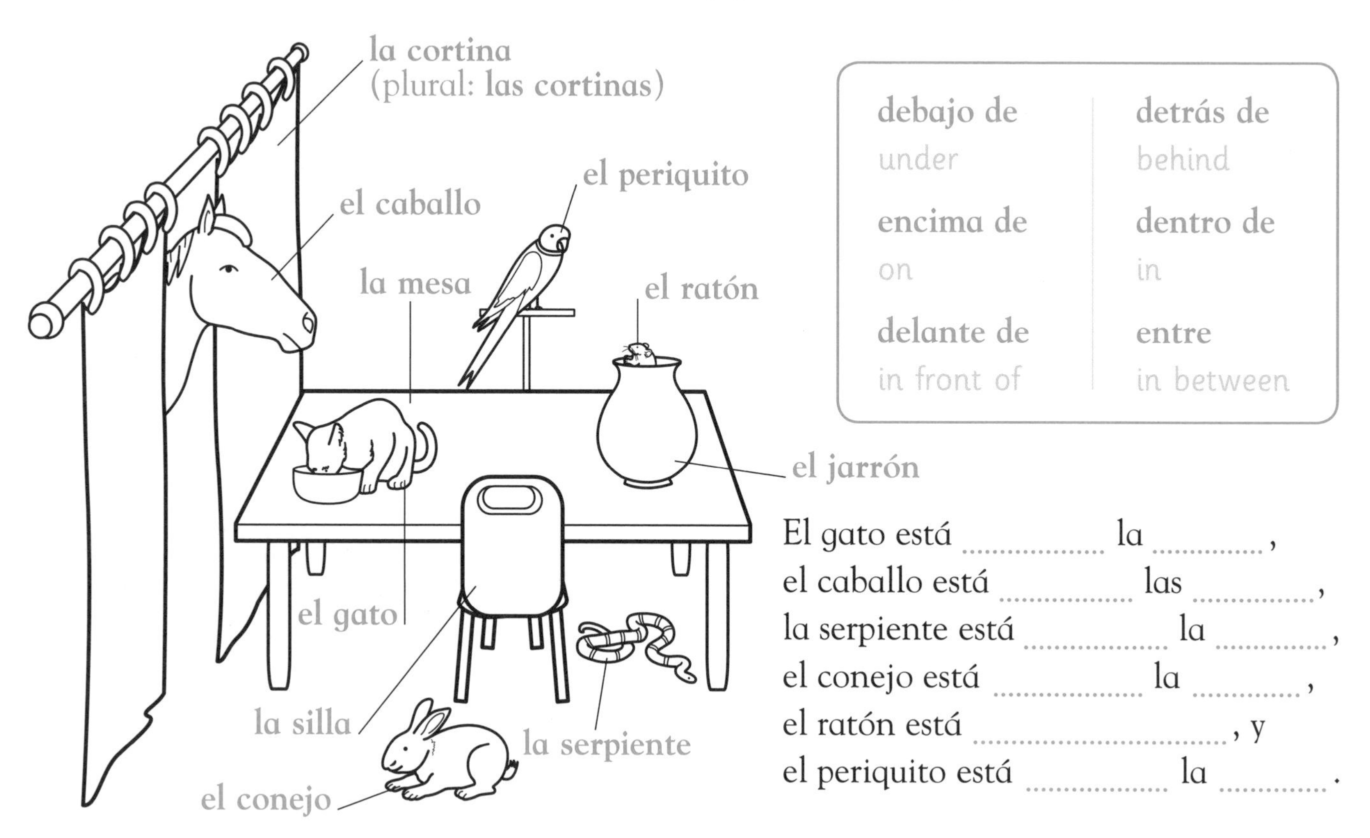

debajo de under	**detrás de** behind
encima de on	**dentro de** in
delante de in front of	**entre** in between

El gato está .... la ....,
el caballo está .... las ....,
la serpiente está .... la ....,
el conejo está .... la ....,
el ratón está ...., y
el periquito está .... la ....

Practise asking for and giving directions, using the map and sentences given below. Use a dictionary or the Internet to look up words you do not know.

Disculpe. ¿Dónde está la piscina?
Excuse me. Where is the swimming pool?

Tome la primera calle a la izquierda/ derecha.
Take the first road on the left/right.

Tome la segunda calle a la izquierda/ derecha.
Take the second road on the left/right.

Está a su izquierda/ derecha.
It is on your left/right.

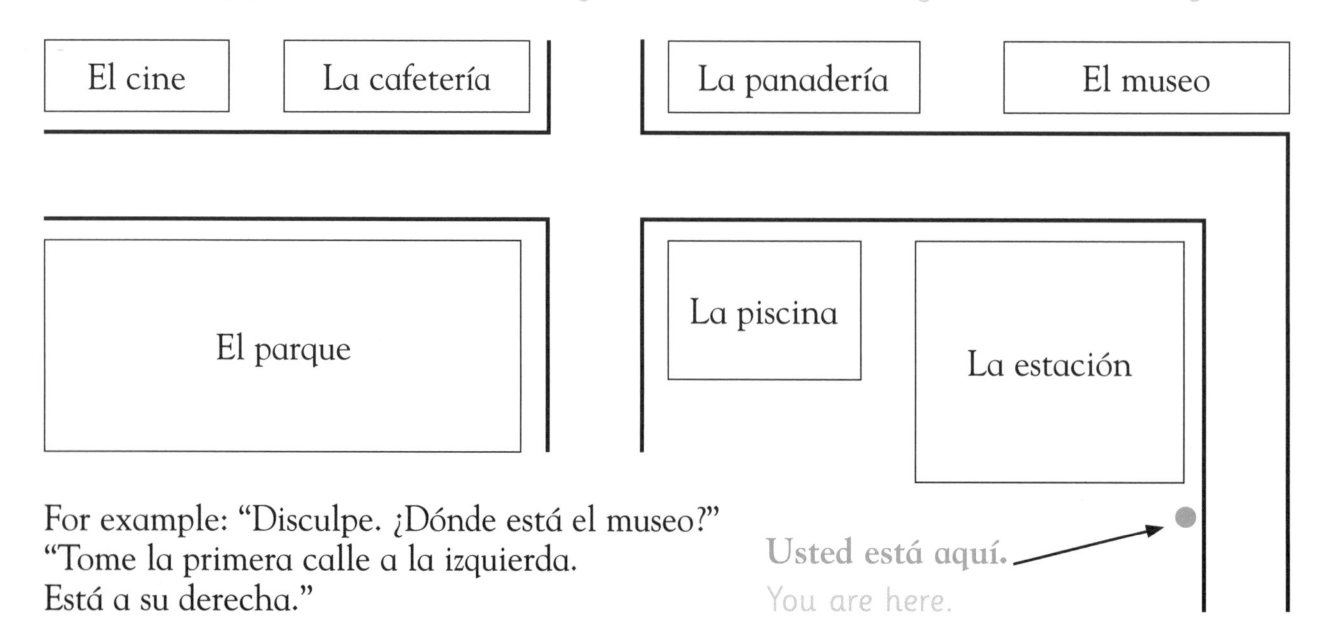

For example: "Disculpe. ¿Dónde está el museo?"
"Tome la primera calle a la izquierda.
Está a su derecha."

Usted está aquí.
You are here.

Los números 20–60

To make numbers over thirty, combine tens and units with a y, instead of the dash in English. For example:

treinta y ocho

thirty-eight

But watch out for the twenties which are slightly different:

veintiuno, veintidós, veintitrés, veinticuatro, veinticinco, veintiséis, veintisiete, veintiocho, veintinueve

Read out the numbers shown below.

veinte	treinta	cuarenta	cincuenta	sesenta
20	30	40	50	60

Count the number of blocks and write the number in Spanish below it.

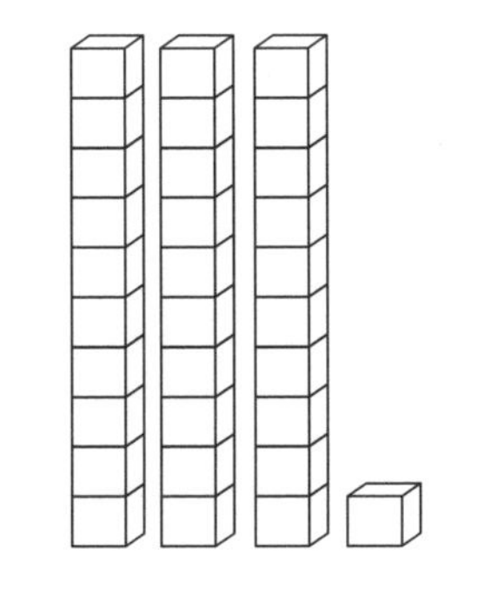

....

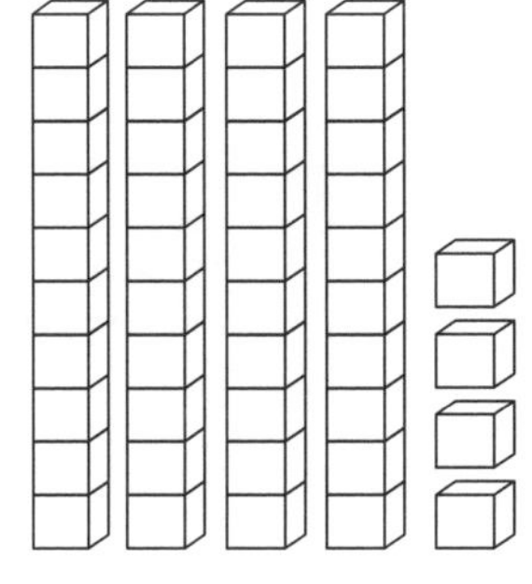

....

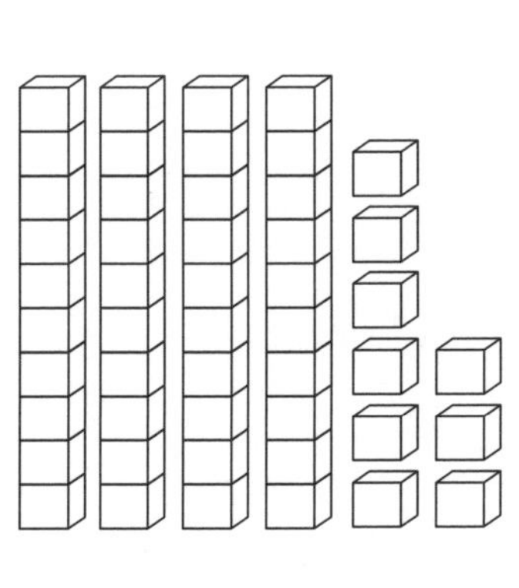

....

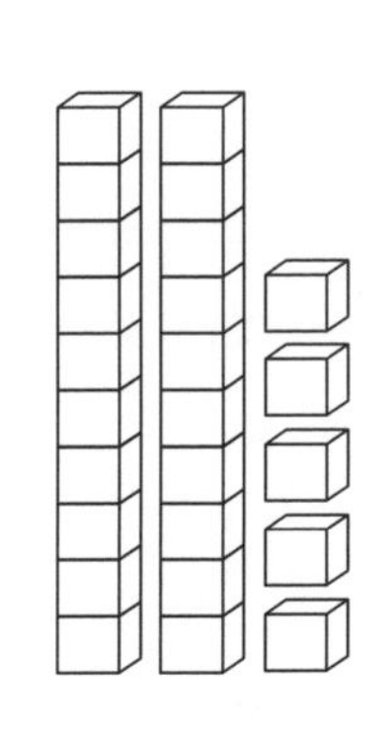

....

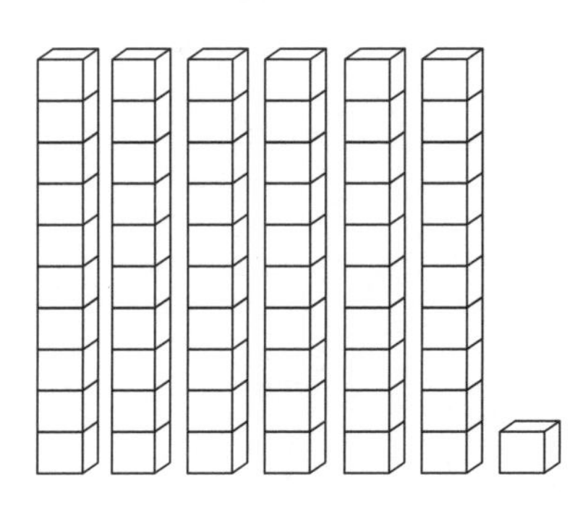

....

Write the answer to the following sums in Spanish.

diez + veinte = ...

cincuenta – cuarenta = ...

cincuenta – diez = ...

cuarenta – veinte = ...

sesenta + cinco = ...

cuarenta – cinco = ...

Señor Buho says, "Keep practising numbers. Try counting backwards, counting in steps of two or clapping a rhythm."

¿Qué tiempo hace?

Look at the key below. Read out the phrases describing the weather.

Hace buen tiempo.
The weather is good.

Hace calor.
It is hot.

Llueve.
It is raining.

Hay tormenta.
It is stormy.

Hace mal tiempo.
The weather is bad.

Hace frío.
It is cold.

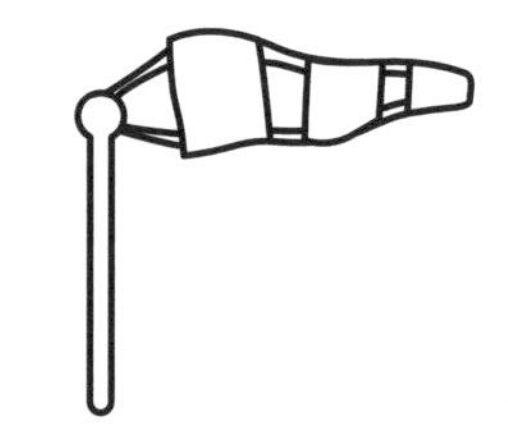

Hace viento.
It is windy.

Nieva.
It is snowing.

Now use the map, key and compass points to complete the weather report.

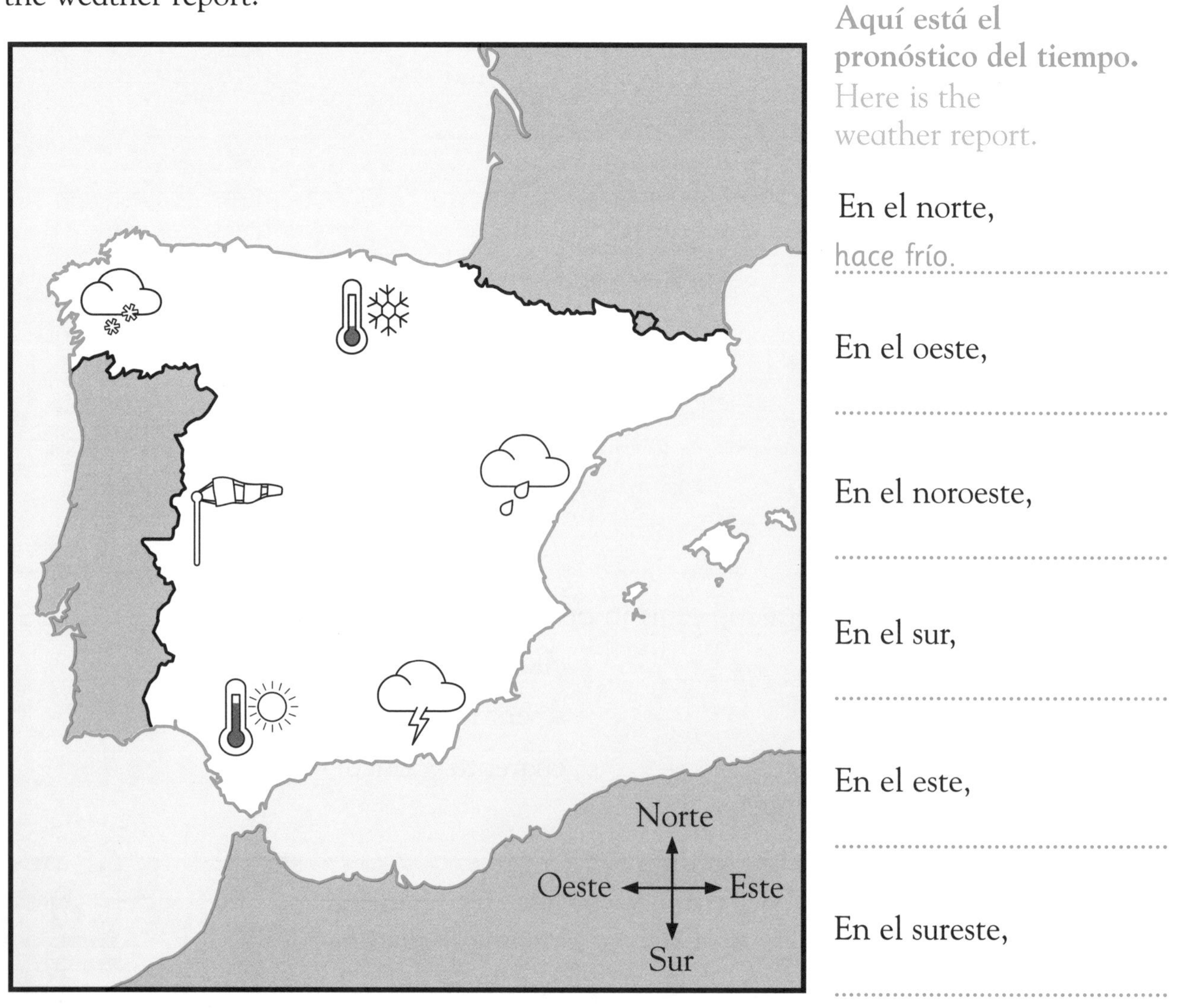

Aquí está el pronóstico del tiempo.
Here is the weather report.

En el norte,
hace frío. ....

En el oeste,
....

En el noroeste,
....

En el sur,
....

En el este,
....

En el sureste,
....

Los días de la semana

Here are the days of the week in Spanish. Read them out loud.

lunes Monday

martes Tuesday

miércoles Wednesday

jueves Thursday

viernes Friday

sábado Saturday

domingo Sunday

Remember that the days of the week in Spanish always start with a small letter.

Now read these sentences.

¿Qué día es hoy?
What is the date today?

Hoy, es domingo 15 de agosto.
Today, it is Sunday, 15th August.

Complete this sentence with today's date.

Hoy, es ....

Keep a weather diary for a week. Write a phrase to describe the weather for each day. For example:

Hoy, hace sol.
Today it is sunny.

lunes	martes	miércoles	jueves

viernes	sábado	domingo

¿Dónde vives?

Look at these sentences. Read them out loud. Adapt them to say which city, town or village you live in.

Vivo en Londres.
I live in London.

Vivo en Bristol.
I live in Bristol.

What kind of place do you live in? Is it big or small? Is it in town or in the country, by the sea or in the mountains? Use these sentences to describe it.

Vivo en una aldea.
I live in a village.

Vivo en una ciudad.
I live in a city.

Vivo en un pueblo.
I live in a town.

Vivo en las afueras.
I live in the suburbs.

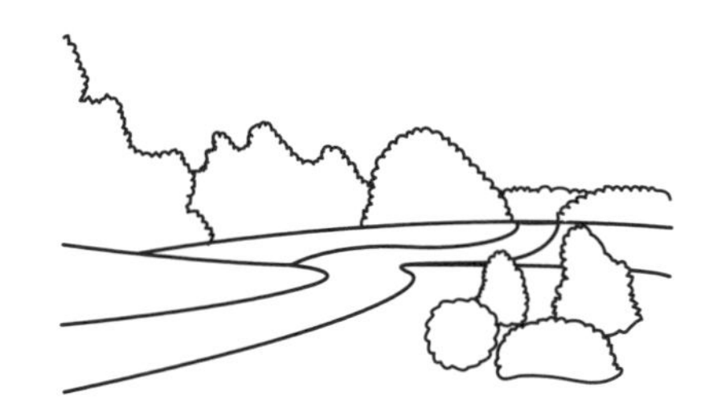

Vivo en el campo.
I live in the country.

Vivo cerca del mar.
I live by the sea.

Vivo en las montañas.
I live in the mountains.

Now translate these English sentences.

I live in Camden. ....

I live in a town by the sea. ....

I live in the country. ....

I live in the suburbs. ....

I live in a village in the mountains. ....

Los verbos -ir

Verbs are doing words. Some Spanish verbs end with the letters 'ir'. An example is **vivir**/to live. Study the chart below to see how verb endings change, depending on who the doer of the verb is.

Yo	vivo	I live
Tú	vives	You live
Él	vive	He lives
Ella	vive	She lives
Nosotros	vivimos	We live
Vosotros	vivís	You live
Ellos	viven	They live
Ellas	viven	They live

Why do you think there are two ways of saying 'you' and two ways of saying 'they'?

....

....

....

Look at the phrases and pictures below.

en un piso
in an apartment

en una casa
in a house

en una granja
on a farm

Build the sentences below to fit the pictures.
Use the phrases given on this page and page 24.

Vivimos ....

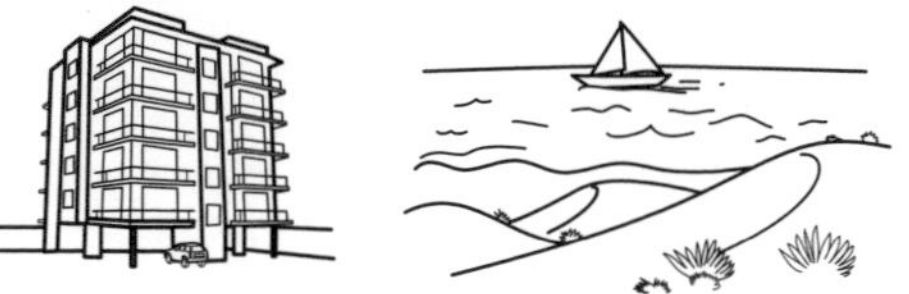

Vivís ....

Viven ....

La casa

Here are some of the rooms you will find in a house.

un salón
a sitting room

un cuarto de baño
a bathroom

una cocina
a kitchen

una habitación de los niños
a nursery

un comedor
a dining room

un dormitorio
a bedroom

en la segunda planta
on the second floor

en la primera planta
on the first floor

en la planta baja
on the ground floor

Imagine you are selling this house. Write a short description of what there is on each floor. Start by writing: **En la planta baja, hay...** / On the ground floor, there is...

....

....

....

Can you describe the rooms in your home? Start by writing:
En mi casa, hay... / In my house, there is...

....

....

....

....

Here are the Spanish words for various types of clothing.

un abrigo a coat	**un jersey** a jumper	**unos vaqueros** some jeans
un gorro a hat	**una bufanda** a scarf	**unos guantes** some gloves
una camiseta a t-shirt	**una falda** a skirt	**un vestido** a dress
unas gafas de sol some sunglasses	**unas botas** some boots	**unos zapatos** some shoes

From the list above, pick out suitable clothes for the weather described in the following sentences. Use them to complete the sentences. For example:

Hace frío. Voy a llevar un abrigo y una bufanda.
It is cold. I am going to wear a coat and a scarf.

Nieva. Voy a llevar ....

Hace calor. Voy a llevar ....

Hace sol. Voy a llevar ....

Tonight it is the school disco. Draw what you plan to wear. Describe your outfit. Start with:
Esta noche, voy a llevar... / Tonight, I am going to wear...

Esta noche, voy a llevar ....

Los pasatiempos

Look at these activities. Can you work out from the pictures what they are in English?

jugar al fútbol

montar a caballo

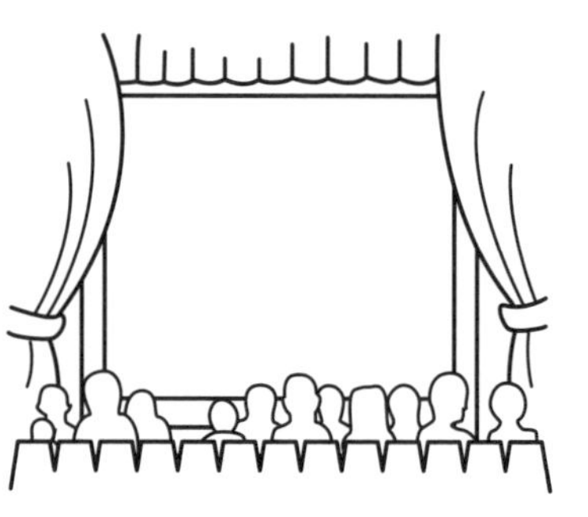

ir al cine

jugar al ordenador

ir a la piscina

montar en bici

Sophie is going on an activity holiday. Unscramble the activities (in brackets) in the programme below to plan her week. The first one has been done for you.

El lunes, va (al a nicapis) a la piscina.

El martes, va a (ne tarmon cibi) ....

El miércoles, va a (a ollabac nomtar) ....

El jueves, va a (la bolfút garju) ....

El viernes, va (neci la) ....

¿Y tú? ¿Qué vas a hacer el próximo fin de semana?

And you? What are you going to do next weekend?

El sábado, voy a ....

El domingo, voy a ....

Use the phrases about activities to say what you like and do not like doing.

For example: **Me gusta montar a caballo pero no me gusta jugar al ordenador.**
I like horse riding, but I do not like playing computer games.

Me gusta .... pero no me gusta ....

Look at the Spanish words for the following numbers.

70 setenta	80 ochenta	90 noventa	100 cien

Read out the numbers given below.

ochenta y uno	cien	noventa
setenta	setenta y dos	ochenta y siete
ochenta y tres	setenta y cinco	ochenta y cinco

Do any of the numbers on the fish in the pond below match those given above? Colour them in.

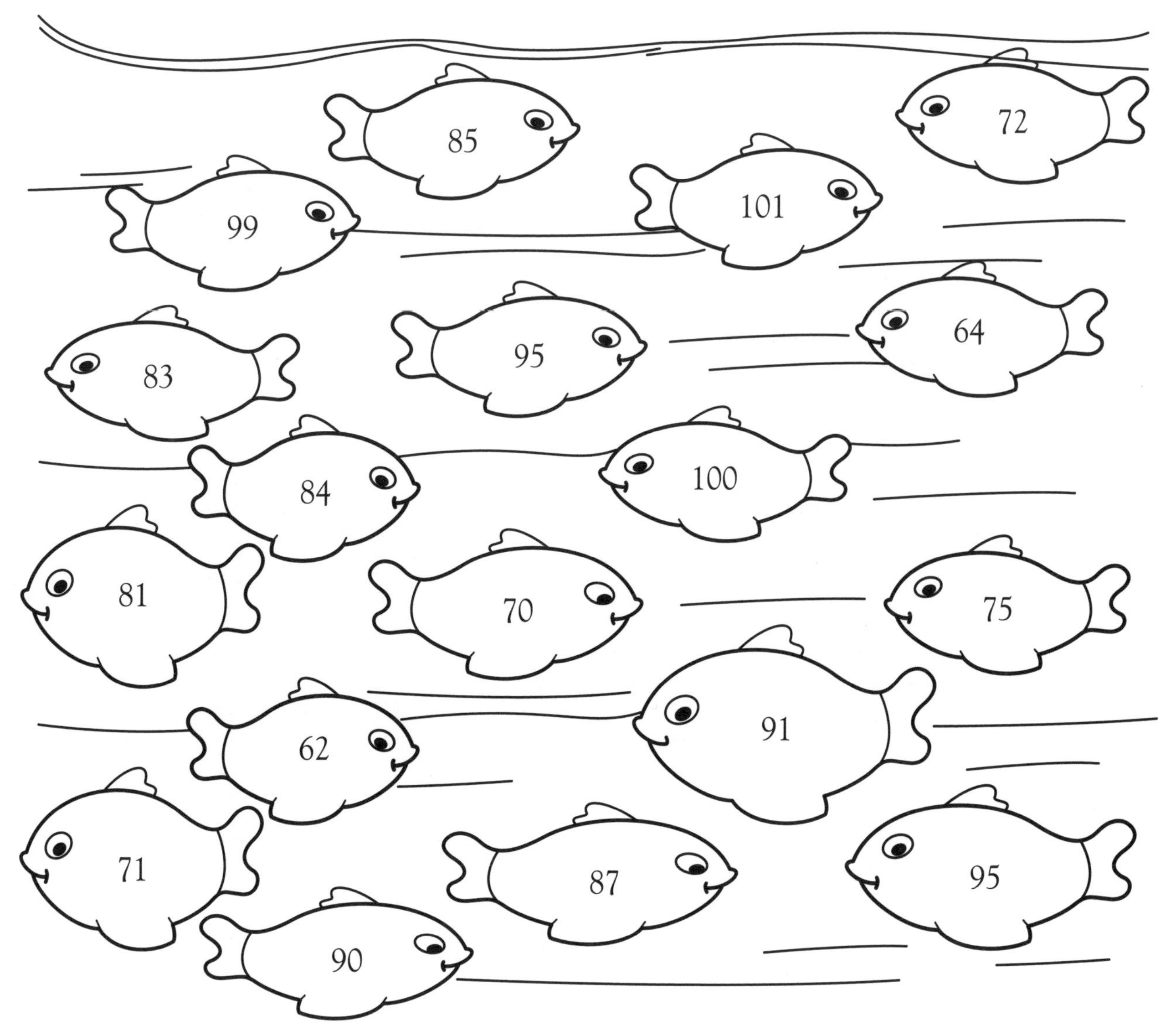

La comida

Here is some of the food you may choose to take on a picnic.

un sandwich de jamón
a ham sandwich

pan
some bread

un pastel de chocolate
a chocolate cake

queso
some cheese

ensalada
some salad

un plátano
a banana

una manzana
an apple

Look at each of the picnic plates below. Use the list of snacks given above to write about what you ate. Start with: **Comí...** / I ate...

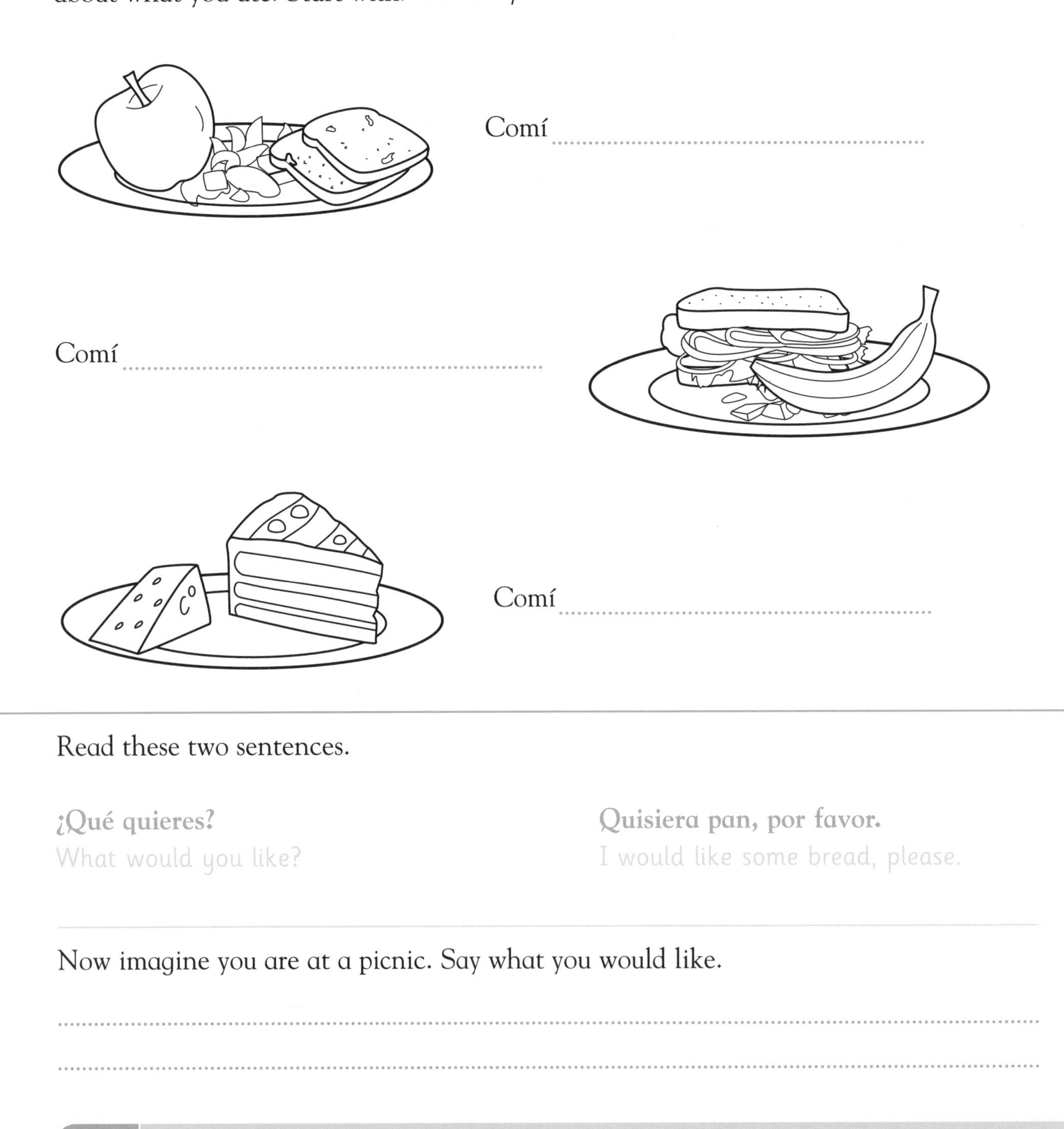

Comí ....

Comí ....

Comí ....

Read these two sentences.

¿Qué quieres?
What would you like?

Quisiera pan, por favor.
I would like some bread, please.

Now imagine you are at a picnic. Say what you would like.

....

....

Here are some of the things you might order in a café or a restaurant.

una porción de pizza a slice of pizza	**un zumo de naranja** an orange juice	**un refresco de cola** a cola
un sandwich de queso a cheese sandwich	**patatas fritas** some chips	**un helado de fresa** a strawberry ice cream

Look at the trays of food below. Then fill in the speech bubble for each order, matching what is on the tray. Start with: **Quisiera...** / I would like...

Read out this list of foods.

el arroz rice	**la carne** meat	**las zanahorias** carrots	**el agua** water
el aceite oil	**la pasta** pasta	**la leche** milk	**la mermelada** jam

At the supermarket, you might have difficulty finding some of them and might have to ask.

¿Tiene?
Do you have...?

Me llevo...
I'll have...

Now translate these sentences.

Do you have any milk? ....

I'll have some oil. ....

Do you have any carrots? ....

I'll have some meat. ....

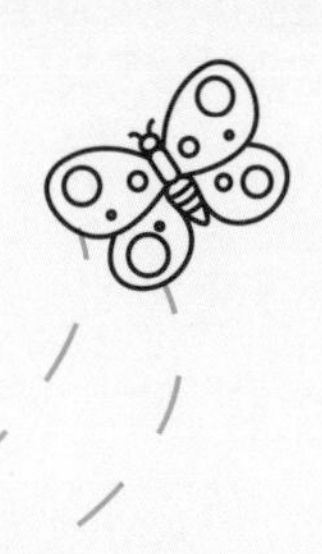

Certificate

Ages 7–11

Congratulations to

....

for successfully finishing this book.

WELL DONE!

You're a star.

☆ ☆ ☆ ☆ ☆

Date

....

Answer section with parents' notes

This book helps to support children's initial understanding of Spanish. The exercises encourage children to take pleasure in and explore language. They also foster curiosity about the customs and culture of another country.

Contents

By working through the activities, your child will practise:

- saying his or her name and greeting people;
- expressing how he or she feels;
- counting from 1–100;
- asking people their age and saying his or her own;
- understanding the gender of nouns;
- describing nouns, using adjectival agreements;
- talking about times and dates, including birthdays;
- expressing preferences (about colours, pets and hobbies);
- describing simple appearances and clothes;
- understanding plural forms and the negative form;
- talking about position and directions;
- discussing the weather;
- understanding the conjugation of verbs;
- using the immediate future and the perfect tense;
- asking for things in shops and restaurants.

How to help your child

The activities in this book help children to express their thoughts in Spanish and understand and respond to other people speaking Spanish. Children need to practise a new language by speaking and writing it. Encourage them to read their responses to exercises aloud, and practise asking questions as well as answering them. Help your child to explore meanings and spellings and to grasp basic language structures. Provide opportunities for further practice to help children begin memorising words and phrases. Also encourage the use of a dictionary to broaden their vocabulary. Have fun adapting words and structures seen here to create new sentences to use in everyday situations at home. Young children have a natural disposition for learning languages. Confidence in language at a young age will support future language learning.

¡Buena suerte!

4

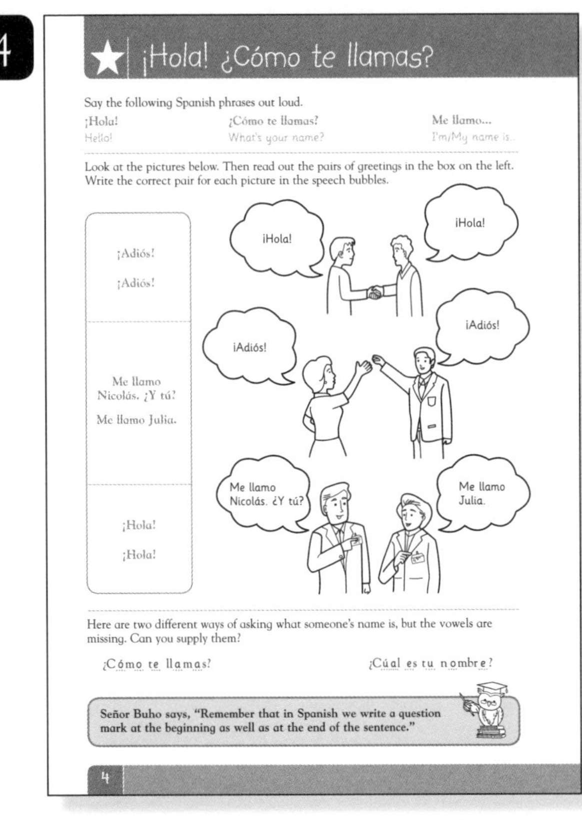

¡Hola! ¿Cómo te llamas?

Say the following Spanish phrases out loud.

¡Hola!	¿Cómo te llamas?	Me llamo...
Hello!	What's your name?	I'm/My name is...

Look at the pictures below. Then read out the pairs of greetings in the box on the left. Write the correct pair for each picture in the speech bubbles.

¡Adiós!
¡Adiós!

Me llamo Nicolás. ¿Y tú?
Me llamo Julia.

¡Hola!
¡Hola!

Here are two different ways of asking what someone's name is, but the vowels are missing. Can you supply them?

¿Cómo te llamas? ¿Cúal es tu nombre?

Señor Buho says, "Remember that in Spanish we write a question mark at the beginning as well as at the end of the sentence."

4

Children should be able to greet each other with confidence. Make sure that children have a chance to practise simple question forms too.

5

¿Qué tal?

Look at these Spanish expressions.

¡Qué tal?	Bien.	Muy bien, gracias.	No muy bien.
How are you?	Fine	Very well, thanks.	Not too well.

Now draw three faces in the box below: one happy and smiling, another looking sad and a third face that simply looks content and relaxed.
Choose an expression from above to match each of the faces you have drawn.

Muy bien, gracias.

Bien.

No muy bien.

¿Y tú? ¿Qué tal?

Answers may vary

Señor Buho says, "In Spanish, we also have a slightly more formal way of saying *How are you?* We say, *¿Cómo estás?*"

5

Children should understand that when they ask a question, they need to raise their voice at the beginning. *¿Cómo te llamas?*, *¿Qué tal ?* and *¿Cuántos años tienes?* are ideal phrases for practising this skill.

6 **7**

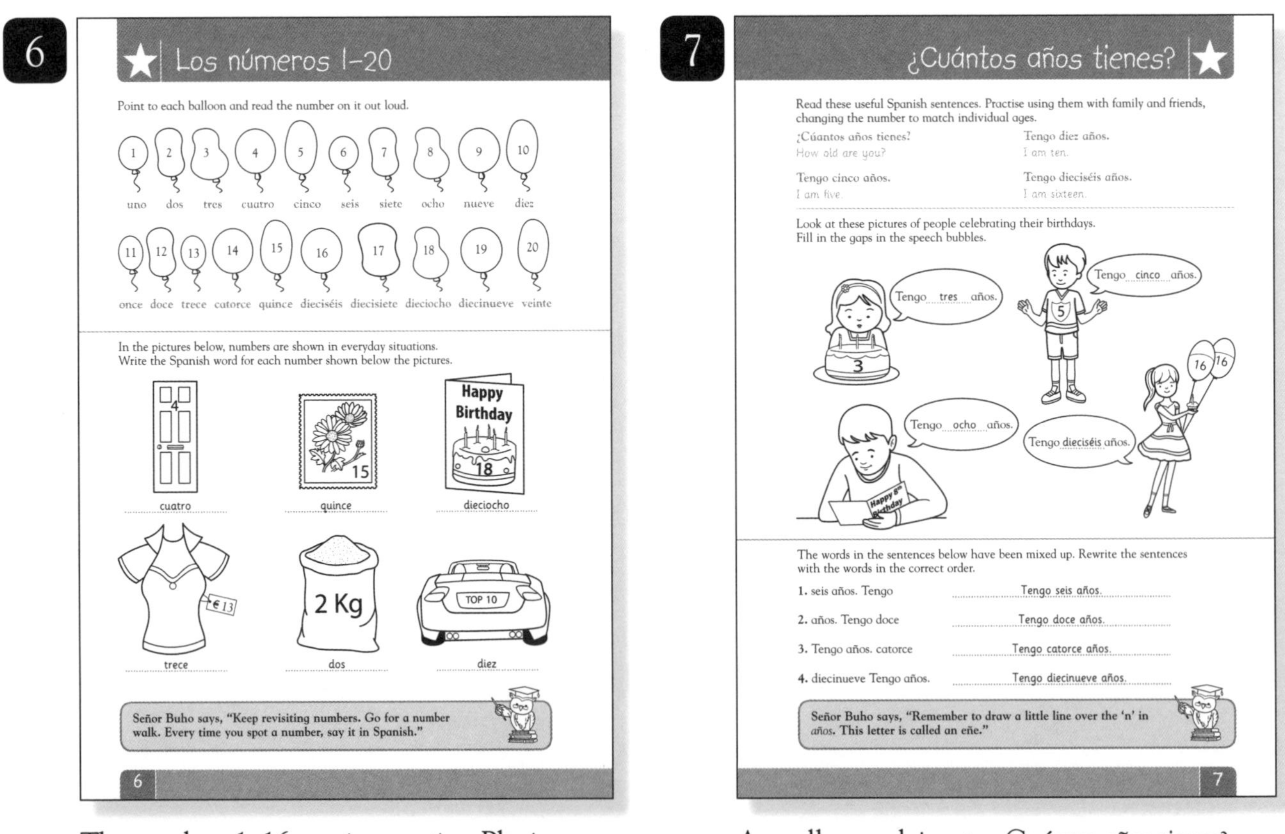

Los números 1–20

Point to each balloon and read the number on it out loud.

1	2	3	4	5	6	7	8	9	10
uno	dos	tres	cuatro	cinco	seis	siete	ocho	nueve	diez

11	12	13	14	15	16	17	18	19	20
once	doce	trece	catorce	quince	dieciséis	diecisiete	dieciocho	diecinueve	veinte

In the pictures below, numbers are shown in everyday situations.
Write the Spanish word for each number shown below the pictures.

cuatro quince dieciocho

trece dos diez

Señor Buho says, "Keep revisiting numbers. Go for a number walk. Every time you spot a number, say it in Spanish."

6

¿Cuántos años tienes?

Read these useful Spanish sentences. Practise using them with family and friends, changing the number to match individual ages.

¿Cuántos años tienes?	Tengo diez años.
How old are you?	I am ten.
Tengo cinco años.	Tengo dieciséis años.
I am five.	I am sixteen.

Look at these pictures of people celebrating their birthdays.
Fill in the gaps in the speech bubbles.

The words in the sentences below have been mixed up. Rewrite the sentences with the words in the correct order.

1. seis años. Tengo — Tengo seis años.
2. años. Tengo doce — Tengo doce años.
3. Tengo años. catorce — Tengo catorce años.
4. diecinueve Tengo años. — Tengo diecinueve años.

Señor Buho says, "Remember to draw a little line over the 'n' in *años*. This letter is called an eñe."

7

The numbers 1–16 require practice. Playing number games such as bingo will help. Understanding the pattern of numbers *dieciséis* (16), *diecisiete* (17), *dieciocho* (18) and *diecinueve* (19) is similar to English 'teens' can be useful.

As well as replying to *¿Cuántos años tienes?*, children need to practise the question form so that they can initiate conversations themselves.

8

En mi estuche

Look at these pictures and read out the labels. Say what you have in your pencil case.

una regla
una calculadora
un bolígrafo
una goma
un lápiz
un rotulador
un sacapuntas

These children are describing the contents of their pencil cases.
Read each description and match it to the correct group of objects shown below.

Tengo una goma y dos lápices.
Tengo un bolígrafo y una regla.
Tengo una calculadora y tres rotuladores.

In Spanish, all nouns (things or people) are either masculine or feminine.
The Spanish word for *a* is either *un* or *una*, depending on whether the noun following it is masculine or feminine.

Put the words below in the correct place on the chart.

un bolígrafo, una goma, una regla, un lápiz, un rotulador, una calculadora

Masculine	Feminine
un bolígrafo	una goma
un lápiz	una regla
un rotulador	una calculadora

8

This is the first collection of nouns and a useful opportunity for talking about the gender of nouns. Draw children's attention to *un* and *una* used for different nouns and compare against *a*/*an* in English.

9

Los adjetivos

Adjectives are used to describe people or things. Here are some useful Spanish adjectives you may use to describe yourself or your friends.

simpático/simpática
pequeño/pequeña
glotón/glotona
hablador/habladora
perezoso/perezosa
deportista

Answer the following question. Use any adjectives you know, including those given above, in your reply.

¿Cómo eres? Soy ....
What are you like? I am .... Answers may vary

Remember that adjectives in Spanish 'agree' with the object or person they are describing. Fill in the missing words on the chart below.

English	Masculine Adjective	Feminine Adjective
sporty	deportista	deportista
lazy	perezoso	perezosa
talkative	hablador	habladora
small	pequeño	pequeña
greedy	glotón	glotona
nice	simpático	simpática

9

Now that children know about gender, they can begin to use adjectives that agree with nouns. Point to the different spellings of masculine and feminine adjectives and ask children how the spelling has changed.

10

Los meses del año

Read out the list of months in the box on the right. Then look at the pictures below. Circle the month that best matches each picture.

(noviembre) agosto
junio (enero)
abril (diciembre)
(febrero) julio
(octubre) marzo
(mayo) septiembre

enero
febrero
marzo
abril
mayo
junio
julio
agosto
septiembre
octubre
noviembre
diciembre

Read these sentences.

Mi cumpleaños es el 4 de julio.
My birthday is on the 4th of July.

El cumpleaños de Sofía es el 8 de febrero.
Sofia's birthday is on the 8th of February.

Now look at the notes from a Birthday Book on the left.
Use the information given to complete these sentences.

BIRTHDAYS
Julie 18th March
Thomas 4th June
David 17th August
Sam 10th May

El cumpleaños de Julie es el 18 de marzo.
El cumpleaños de Thomas es el 4 de junio.
El cumpleaños de David es el 17 de agosto.
El cumpleaños de Sam es el 10 de mayo.

¿Y tú? ¿Cuándo es tu cumpleaños?
And you? When is your birthday?
Answers may vary

Señor Buho says, "In Spanish, months begin with a small letter, for example, *abril*. English uses a capital letter, for example, April."

10

Children will enjoy talking about birthdays and saying more about themselves in Spanish. They can begin by saying which month their birthday is in, e.g. *en enero*, then progress to combining numbers and months.

11

¿Qué hora es?

Read out the times shown on the clock faces below.

7:00 Son las siete.
7:15 Son las siete y cuarto.
11:30 Son las once y media.
8:45 Son las nueve menos cuarto.

Read each sentence. Then circle the clock face above it showing that time.

Son las dos y media.
Son las cuatro menos cuarto.
Son las seis y cuarto.

12:30 02:00 Son las dos.
09:45 08:45 Son las nueve menos cuarto.
01:30 01:00 Es la una y media.

Look at the phrases and pictures below.

a mediodía – at midday
a las once – at eleven o'clock
a las cinco y cuarto – at quarter past five
a medianoche – at midnight

Me despierto.
Me lavo.
Desayuno.
Me lavo los dientes.

Read the sentences below, describing regular morning activities. The times given are unusual. Rewrite each sentence, using times that match your morning routine.

Me despierto a las once.
Me lavo a las once y media.
Desayuno a mediodía.
Me lavo los dientes a las cinco y cuarto.

Answers may vary

11

It is a good idea to reinforce children's numbers 1–12 before practising the time. Start by telling the time on the hour before progressing to half-hours and quarter-hours. Make sure children practise the question form.

12

Los colores

Here is a list of colours.

blanco	white	amarillo	yellow	marrón	brown
negro	black	verde	green	gris	grey
azul	blue	rosa	pink	naranja	orange
rojo	red	morado	purple		

Read the names of the colours out loud, then select from them to complete the sentences below.

Un elefante es gris.
El cielo es azul.
El chocolate es marrón.
La leche es blanca.
Una naranja es naranja.
El limón es amarillo.

Answer the following question.

¿Cuál es tu color favorito? Mi color favorito es ....
What is your favourite colour? My favourite colour is Answers may vary

Señor Buho says, "Compare new Spanish words with English words. Sometimes there are similarities that can help you remember them."

12

Provide lots of opportunity to practise colours. It is a good idea to start with six colours and build from there. Children will enjoy listening to a colour sequence and repeating it.

13

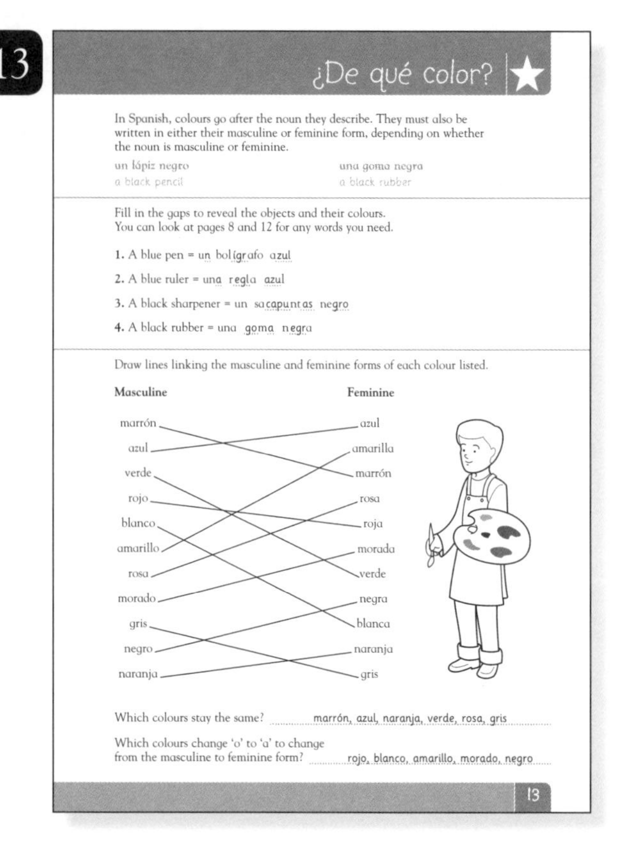

¿De qué color?

In Spanish, colours go after the noun they describe. They must also be written in either their masculine or feminine form, depending on whether the noun is masculine or feminine.

un lápiz negro — a black pencil
una goma negra — a black rubber

Fill in the gaps to reveal the objects and their colours. You can look at pages 8 and 12 for any words you need.

1. A blue pen = un bolígrafo azul
2. A blue ruler = una regla azul
3. A black sharpener = un sacapuntas negro
4. A black rubber = una goma negra

Draw lines linking the masculine and feminine forms of each colour listed.

Masculine	Feminine
marrón	azul
azul	amarilla
verde	marrón
rojo	rosa
blanco	roja
amarillo	morada
rosa	verde
morado	negra
gris	blanca
negro	naranja
naranja	gris

Which colours stay the same? marrón, azul, naranja, verde, rosa, gris

Which colours change 'o' to 'a' to change from the masculine to feminine form? rojo, blanco, amarillo, morado, negro

13

Colours are a good way of introducing children to adjectives following the noun. It would be useful to compare this page with page 9 where children also thought about adjectival agreement.

14

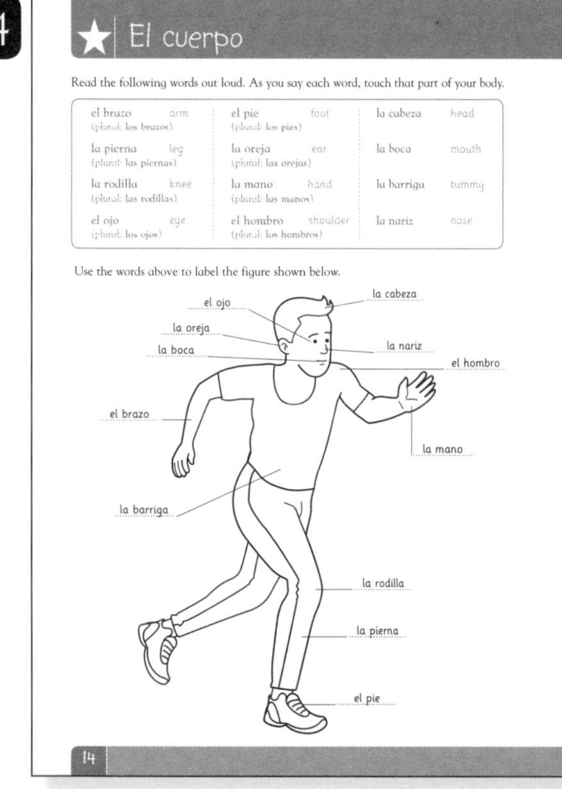

El cuerpo

Read the following words out loud. As you say each word, touch that part of your body.

el brazo (plural: los brazos)	arm	el pie (plural: los pies)	foot	la cabeza	head
la pierna (plural: las piernas)	leg	la oreja (plural: las orejas)	ear	la boca	mouth
la rodilla (plural: las rodillas)	knee	la mano (plural: las manos)	hand	la barriga	tummy
el ojo (plural: los ojos)	eye	el hombro (plural: los hombros)	shoulder	la nariz	nose

Use the words above to label the figure shown below.

14

Point out to children the Spanish for *the* – *el* (m.), *la* (f.), *los* (m. plural) and *las* (f. plural).

15

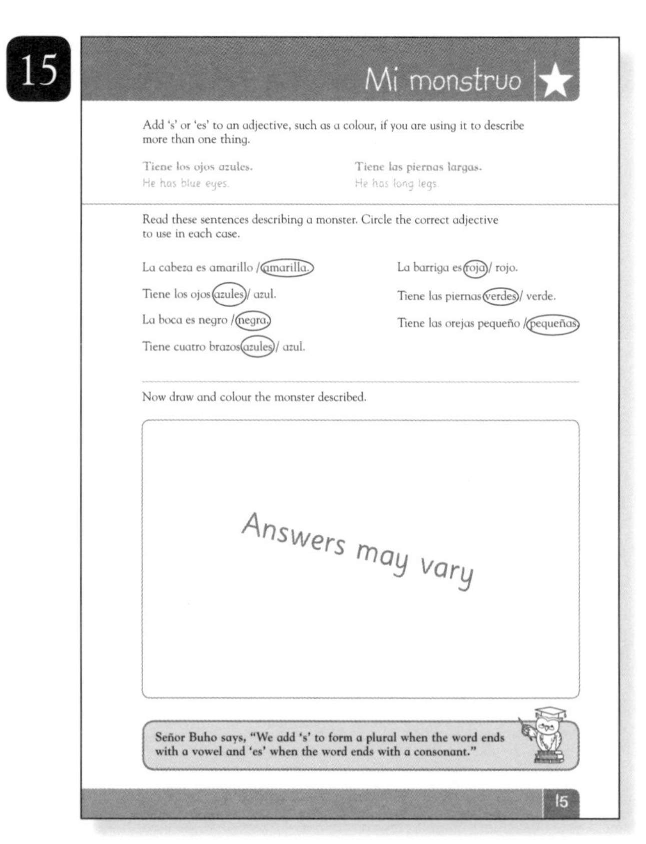

Mi monstruo

Add 's' or 'es' to an adjective, such as a colour, if you are using it to describe more than one thing.

Tiene los ojos azules. — He has blue eyes.
Tiene las piernas largas. — He has long legs.

Read these sentences describing a monster. Circle the correct adjective to use in each case.

La cabeza es amarillo / (amarilla).
Tiene los ojos (azules) / azul.
La boca es negro / (negra).
Tiene cuatro brazos (azules) / azul.
La barriga es (roja) / rojo.
Tiene las piernas (verdes) / verde.
Tiene las orejas pequeño / (pequeñas).

Now draw and colour the monster described.

Answers may vary

Señor Buho says, "We add 's' to form a plural when the word ends with a vowel and 'es' when the word ends with a consonant."

15

Children will need to be confident using the verb *tener*. Compare *Tengo* on page 7 with *Tiene* on this page. Children here gain further practice in adjectival agreement.

16

Los retratos

Read out the following Spanish sentences and phrases.

Tiene los ojos marrones. He has/She has brown eyes.	los ojos verdes green eyes	los ojos azules blue eyes
Tiene el pelo rubio. He has/She has blonde hair.	el pelo negro black hair	Tiene barba. He has a beard
Lleva gafas. He/She wears glasses	el pelo corto short hair	el pelo largo long hair

Now imagine you are the manager of a new pop band, *Los Tres Amigos*. Look at the picture below. Then use the words in the box under the picture to fill in the gaps in the description of your band members.

Cristina Pedro Silvia

barba largo corto y gafas
pelo Ella tiene ojos

Cristina tiene los ojos azules y el pelo largo y rubio. Pedro tiene los ojos marrones y el pelo corto y negro. Tiene barba. Silvia tiene los ojos verdes y el pelo marrón y corto. Ella lleva gafas.

16

Children will make progress by memorising set phrases. Here they again practise *tener*, using *tiene*.

17

Mi familia

Read the following words and phrases.

mi padre my father	mi madre my mother	Se llama... He/She is called..	Se llaman... They are called..
un hermano a brother	una hermana a sister	No tengo hermanos. I don't have any sisters or brothers.	
Soy... I am..	Es... He is..	Es... She is...	

Read this extract from a letter to a penpal. Then decide if the statements on the chart are true (*verdadero*) or false (*falso*). Tick (✓) the right column. Look up any words you do not know in a dictionary or on the Internet.

En mi familia hay cinco personas. Mi padre se llama Pedro. Es alto y divertido. Mi madre, Susana, es baja y habladora. Tengo dos hermanas que se llaman Sofía y Julia. Sofía tiene cinco años y es tímida. Julia tiene nueve años. Julia tiene el pelo rubio y largo. ¡Es muy perezosa! Para terminar, me llamo David. Tengo siete años. Tengo los ojos verdes y llevo gafas. Mi cumpleaños es el once de julio. Soy deportista y un poco glotón. ¿Y tú? ¿Tienes hermanos?

	Verdadero	Falso
1. There are 4 people in the family.		✓
2. The father is called Pedro.	✓	
3. The mother is talkative.	✓	
4. David has a sister and a brother.		✓
5. Sofía is 9 years old.		✓
6. Julia has long blonde hair.	✓	
7. Julia is shy.		✓
8. David is a bit greedy.	✓	
9. David has blue eyes and wears glasses.		✓
10. David's birthday is on 11 July.	✓	

Señor Buho says, "There are two different ways of saying *my*. Use *mi* in front of a singular noun and *mis* in front of a plural noun."

17

Children need to be confident using the verb *ser*. Compare *soy* against *es* .The reading extract is a good exercise for children to use previous knowledge to determine meaning.

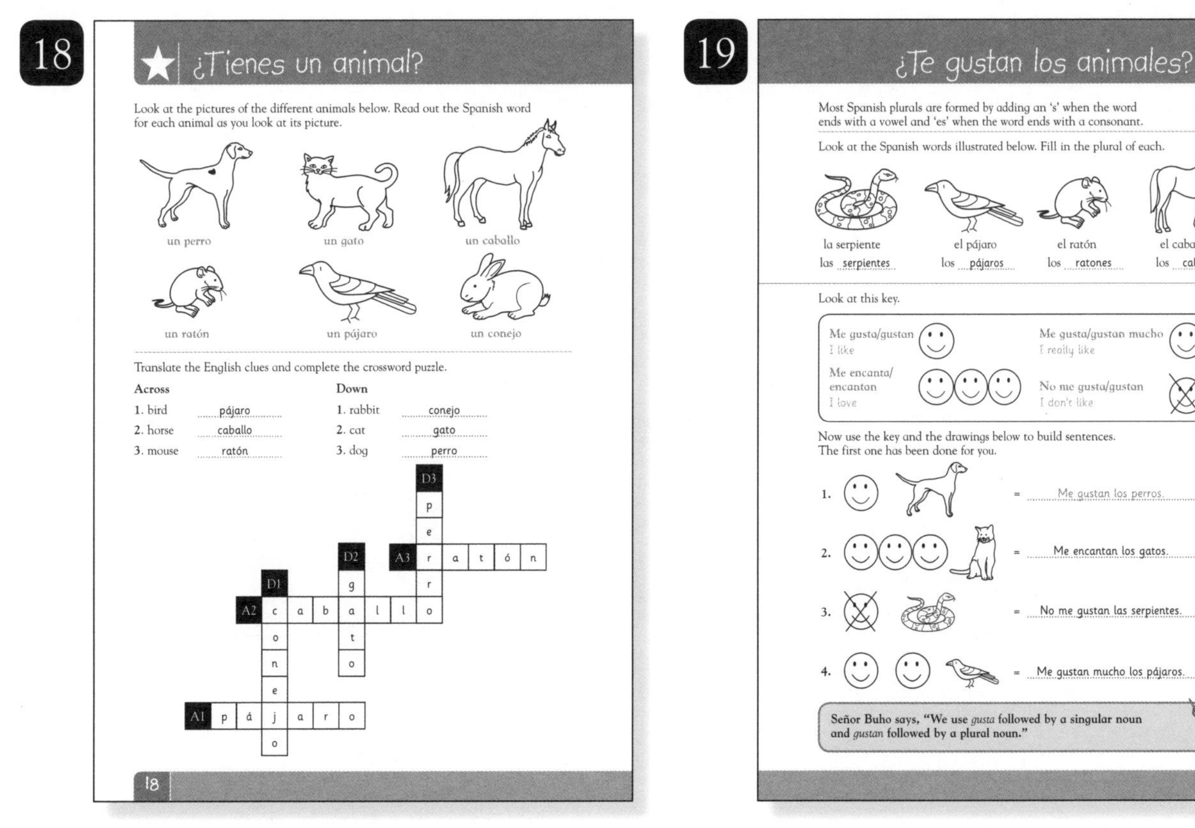

18

¿Tienes un animal?

Look at the pictures of the different animals below. Read out the Spanish word for each animal as you look at its picture.

un perro un gato un caballo
un ratón un pájaro un conejo

Translate the English clues and complete the crossword puzzle.

Across		Down	
1. bird	pájaro	1. rabbit	conejo
2. horse	caballo	2. cat	gato
3. mouse	ratón	3. dog	perro

18

19

¿Te gustan los animales?

Most Spanish plurals are formed by adding an 's' when the word ends with a vowel and 'es' when the word ends with a consonant.

Look at the Spanish words illustrated below. Fill in the plural of each.

la serpiente	el pájaro	el ratón	el caballo
las serpientes	los pájaros	los ratones	los caballos

Look at this key.

Me gusta/gustan I like	Me gusta/gustan mucho I really like
Me encanta/encantan I love	No me gusta/gustan I don't like

Now use the key and the drawings below to build sentences. The first one has been done for you.

1. = Me gustan los perros.
2. = Me encantan los gatos.
3. = No me gustan las serpientes.
4. = Me gustan mucho los pájaros.

Señor Buho says, "We use *gusta* followed by a singular noun and *gustan* followed by a plural noun."

19

Children gain further practice of *tener*, here including the question form *¿Tienes un animal?*. Keep reminding children about the gender of nouns.

Children enjoy expressing preferences. Here they are introduced to *Me gusta/gustan* and the negative *No me gusta/gustan*, which they could progress to applying to different contexts in the book, such as clothes and snacks.

20

¿Dónde está?

Look at the picture. The pets in this house are on the loose! Use the labels and position words in the box on the right to fill in the gaps in the description of the scene.

la cortina (plural: las cortinas)
el caballo
el periquito
la mesa
el ratón
el jarrón
el gato
la silla
la serpiente
el conejo

debajo de	detrás de
under	behind
encima de	dentro de
on	in
delante de	entre
in front of	in between

El gato está encima de la mesa,
el caballo está entre las cortinas,
la serpiente está debajo de la mesa,
el conejo está delante de la silla,
el ratón está dentro del jarrón, y
el periquito está detrás de la mesa.

Practise asking for and giving directions, using the map and sentences given below. Use a dictionary or the Internet to look up words you do not know.

Disculpe. ¿Dónde está la piscina?	Tome la primera calle a la izquierda/derecha.	Tome la segunda calle a la izquierda/derecha.	Está a su izquierda/derecha.
Excuse me. Where is the swimming pool?	Take the first road on the left/right.	Take the second road on the left/right.	It is on your left/right.

El cine
La cafetería
La panadería
El museo
El parque
La piscina
La estación

For example: "Disculpe. ¿Dónde está el museo?"
"Tome la primera calle a la izquierda.
Está a su derecha."

Usted está aquí.
You are here.

20

Children practise *Disculpe* for politely asking questions. Encourage children to research additional vocabulary using a dictionary or the Internet. This a key skill in language learning.

21

Los números 20–60

To make numbers over thirty, combine tens and units with a y, instead of the dash in English. For example:
treinta y ocho
thirty-eight

But watch out for the twenties which are slightly different:
veintiuno, veintidós, veintitrés, veinticuatro, veinticinco, veintiséis, veintisiete, veintiocho, veintinueve

Read out the numbers shown below.

veinte	treinta	cuarenta	cincuenta	sesenta
20	30	40	50	60

Count the number of blocks and write the number in Spanish below it.

treinta y uno
cincuenta y dos
cuarenta y cuatro
cuarenta y nueve
veinticinco
sesenta y uno

Write the answer to the following sums in Spanish.

diez + veinte = treinta
cincuenta – cuarenta = diez
cincuenta – diez = cuarenta
cuarenta – veinte = veinte
sesenta + cinco = sesenta y cinco
cuarenta – cinco = treinta y cinco

Señor Buho says, "Keep practising numbers. Try counting backwards, counting in steps of two or clapping a rhythm."

21

For numbers such as 31 and 41, children need reminding to say y, which helps with pronunciation. They can practise these higher numbers by talking about birthdays, counting everyday objects and playing games.

22

¿Qué tiempo hace?

Look at the key below. Read out the phrases describing the weather.

Hace buen tiempo.	Hace calor.	Llueve.	Hay tormenta.
The weather is good	It is hot	It is raining	It is stormy
Hace mal tiempo.	Hace frío.	Hace viento.	Nieva.
The weather is bad	It is cold	It is windy	It is snowing

Now use the map, key and compass points to complete the weather report.

Norte
Oeste
Este
Sur

Aquí está el pronóstico del tiempo.
Here is the weather report.

En el norte, hace frío.
En el oeste, hace viento.
En el noroeste, nieva.
En el sur, hace calor.
En el este, llueve.
En el sureste, hay tormenta.

22

Familiarise children with compass points by saying directions, turning and pointing. Children should turn to face the same direction. Creating weather maps and pretending to be weather presenters can be fun.

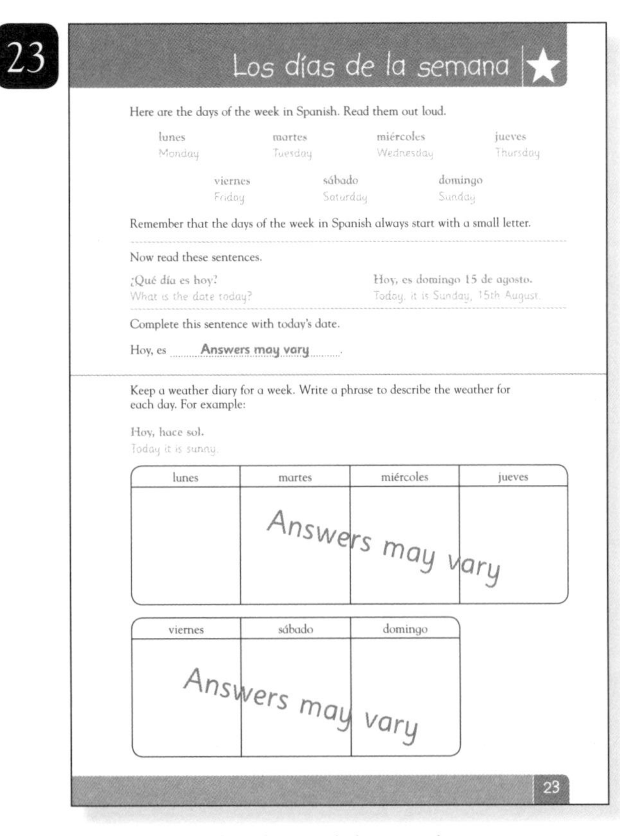
23

Los días de la semana

Here are the days of the week in Spanish. Read them out loud.

lunes	martes	miércoles	jueves
Monday	Tuesday	Wednesday	Thursday
viernes	sábado	domingo	
Friday	Saturday	Sunday	

Remember that the days of the week in Spanish always start with a small letter.

Now read these sentences.

¿Qué día es hoy?
What is the date today?

Hoy, es domingo 15 de agosto.
Today, it is Sunday, 15th August.

Complete this sentence with today's date.

Hoy, es Answers may vary.

Keep a weather diary for a week. Write a phrase to describe the weather for each day. For example:

Hoy, hace sol.
Today it is sunny.

lunes	martes	miércoles	jueves
Answers may vary			

viernes	sábado	domingo
Answers may vary		

23

Try writing the days of the week on paper, jumbling and re-ordering them. Children can consolidate learning here by giving a full weather report and saying the day, date and weather for different regions.

24

¿Dónde vives?

Look at these sentences. Read them out loud. Adapt them to say which city, town or village you live in.

Vivo en Londres. — I live in London.

Vivo en Bristol. — I live in Bristol.

What kind of place do you live in? Is it big or small? Is it in town or in the country, by the sea or in the mountains? Use these sentences to describe it.

Vivo en una aldea. — I live in a village.

Vivo en una ciudad. — I live in a city.

Vivo en un pueblo. — I live in a town.

Vivo en las afueras. — I live in the suburbs.

Vivo en el campo. — I live in the country.

Vivo cerca del mar. — I live by the sea.

Vivo en las montañas. — I live in the mountains.

Now translate these English sentences.

I live in Camden.	Vivo en Camden.
I live in a town by the sea.	Vivo en un pueblo cerca del mar.
I live in the country.	Vivo en el campo.
I live in the suburbs.	Vivo en las afueras.
I live in a village in the mountains.	Vivo en una aldea en las montañas.

24

The phrases here will give children further opportunities to initiate conversation and say more about themselves. Point out that *in* is *en* in Spanish.

25

Los verbos -ir

Verbs are doing words. Some Spanish verbs end with the letters 'ir'. An example is vivir/to live. Study the chart below to see how verb endings change, depending on who the doer of the verb is.

Yo	vivo	I live
Tú	vives	You live
Él	vive	He lives
Ella	vive	She lives
Nosotros	vivimos	We live
Vosotros	vivís	You live
Ellos	viven	They live
Ellas	viven	They live

Why do you think there are two ways of saying 'you' and two ways of saying 'they'?

Tú is singular and vosotros is plural.

Ellos is masculine and ellas is feminine, but for a mixed group, you also use ellos.

Look at the phrases and pictures below.

en un piso — in an apartment

en una casa — in a house

en una granja — on a farm

Build the sentences below to fit the pictures.
Use the phrases given on this page and page 24.

Vivimos en una granja en las montañas.

Vivís en un piso cerca del mar.

Viven en una casa en el campo.

25

Children are introduced to the present tense of a regular -ir verb. The different forms are very different from English. Ask children which letters have been added to *viv* for each form (*yo*, *tú*, *él* etc.).

26

La casa

Here are some of the rooms you will find in a house.

un salón a sitting room	un cuarto de baño a bathroom	una cocina a kitchen
una habitación de los niños a nursery	un comedor a dining room	un dormitorio a bedroom

en la segunda planta — on the second floor

en la primera planta — on the first floor

en la planta baja — on the ground floor

Imagine you are selling this house. Write a short description of what there is on each floor. Start by writing: En la planta baja, hay... / On the ground floor, there is...

En la planta baja, hay un salón, un comedor y una cocina.
En la primera planta, hay dos dormitorios. En la segunda planta, hay una habitación de los niños y un cuarto de baño.

Can you describe the rooms in your home? Start by writing:
En mi casa, hay... / In my house, there is...

Answers may vary

26

Children have the opportunity to write a short text of their own and practise the words *hay* (*there is/there are*) and *y* (*and*). Children could revise numbers and plurals here too.

27

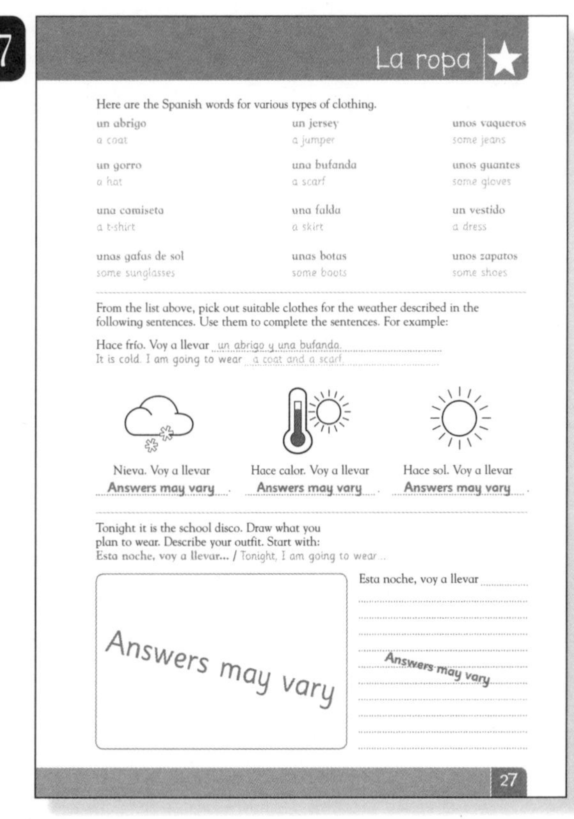

La ropa

Here are the Spanish words for various types of clothing.

un abrigo a coat	un jersey a jumper	unos vaqueros some jeans
un gorro a hat	una bufanda a scarf	unos guantes some gloves
una camiseta a t-shirt	una falda a skirt	un vestido a dress
unas gafas de sol some sunglasses	unas botas some boots	unos zapatos some shoes

From the list above, pick out suitable clothes for the weather described in the following sentences. Use them to complete the sentences. For example:

Hace frío. Voy a llevar un abrigo y una bufanda.
It is cold. I am going to wear a coat and a scarf.

Nieva. Voy a llevar Answers may vary.

Hace calor. Voy a llevar Answers may vary.

Hace sol. Voy a llevar Answers may vary.

Tonight it is the school disco. Draw what you plan to wear. Describe your outfit. Start with:
Esta noche, voy a llevar... / Tonight, I am going to wear...

Answers may vary

Esta noche, voy a llevar

Answers may vary

27

Point out the use of *unos/unas* (some), used with plural nouns. Children are also introduced to the immediate future tense – *voy a* + an infinitive verb. They will enjoy using known structures here in new contexts.

28

Los pasatiempos

Look at these activities. Can you work out from the pictures what they are in English?

jugar al fútbol — montar a caballo — ir al cine

jugar al ordenador — ir a la piscina — montar en bici

Sophie is going on an activity holiday. Unscramble the activities (in brackets) in the programme below to plan her week. The first one has been done for you.

El lunes, va (al a nicapis) a la piscina.

El martes, va a (ne tarmon cibi) montar en bici.

El miércoles, va a (a ollabac nomtar) montar a caballo.

El jueves, va a (la bolfút garju) jugar al fútbol.

El viernes, va (neci la) al cine.

¿Y tú? ¿Qué vas a hacer el próximo fin de semana?
And you? What are you going to do next weekend?

El sábado, voy a Answers may vary.

El domingo, voy a Answers may vary.

Use the phrases about activities to say what you like and do not like doing.

For example: Me gusta montar a caballo pero no me gusta jugar al ordenador.
I like horse riding, but I do not like playing computer games.

Me gusta Answers may vary pero no me gusta Answers may vary.

28

Children practise further forms of the immediate future tense, for example, *va a*. Point out that *On Monday* translates as *El lunes*, literally *The Monday*. The connective *pero* will allow children to extend their sentences.

29

Los números 70–100

Look at the Spanish words for the following numbers.

70	80	90	100
setenta	ochenta	noventa	cien

Read out the numbers given below.

ochenta y uno — cien — noventa

setenta — setenta y dos — ochenta y siete

ochenta y tres — setenta y cinco — ochenta y cinco

Do any of the numbers on the fish in the pond below match those given above? Colour them in.

85 72 99 101 83 95 64 84 100 81 70 75 62 91 71 87 95 90

29

To learn these higher numbers, children need to combine numbers they have already seen on pages 6 and 21. Children could practise by taking measurements and talking about money (euros and cents).

30

La comida

Here is some of the food you may choose to take on a picnic.

un sandwich de jamón — a ham sandwich
pan — some bread
un pastel de chocolate — a chocolate cake
queso — some cheese
ensalada — some salad
un plátano — a banana
una manzana — an apple

Look at each of the picnic plates below. Use the list of snacks given above to write about what you ate. Start with: Comí... / I ate...

Comí pan, ensalada y una manzana.

Comí un sandwich de jamón y un plátano.

Comí queso y un pastel de chocolate.

Read these two sentences.

¿Qué quieres? — What would you like?

Quisiera pan, por favor. — I would like some bread, please.

Now imagine you are at a picnic. Say what you would like.

Answers may vary

30

Children can practise these phrases at the table. They are introduced to the past tense of a regular -er verb – *comí*. They have further practice speaking in a polite way (see page 20).

31

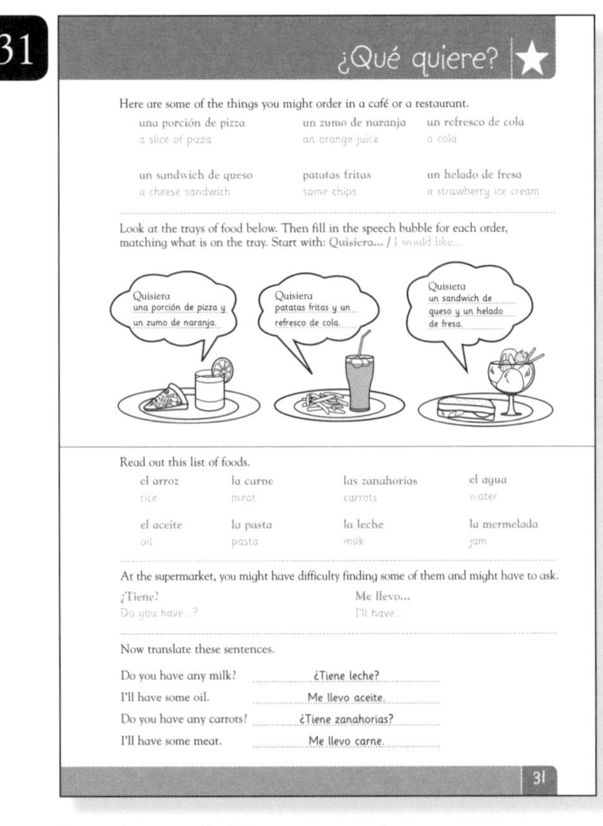

¿Qué quiere?

Here are some of the things you might order in a café or a restaurant.

una porción de pizza — a slice of pizza
un zumo de naranja — an orange juice
un refresco de cola — a cola
un sandwich de queso — a cheese sandwich
patatas fritas — some chips
un helado de fresa — a strawberry ice cream

Look at the trays of food below. Then fill in the speech bubble for each order, matching what is on the tray. Start with: Quisiera... / I would like...

Read out this list of foods.

el arroz — rice
la carne — meat
las zanahorias — carrots
el agua — water
el aceite — oil
la pasta — pasta
la leche — milk
la mermelada — jam

At the supermarket, you might have difficulty finding some of them and might have to ask.

¿Tiene? — Do you have...?

Me llevo... — I'll have...

Now translate these sentences.

Do you have any milk? ¿Tiene leche?

I'll have some oil. Me llevo aceite.

Do you have any carrots? ¿Tiene zanahorias?

I'll have some meat. Me llevo carne.

31

Encourage children to use the structures provided (*Me llevo* and *¿Tiene...?*) and work their way through the whole list of foods.